The Riverside Literature Series

THE SUCCESSION OF FOREST
TREES AND WILD APPLES

BY

HENRY D. THOREAU

WITH A BIOGRAPHICAL SKETCH

BY

RALPH WALDO EMERSON

HOUGHTON, MIFFLIN AND COMPANY

Boston: 4 Park Street; New York: 11 East Seventeenth Street
Chicago: 28 Lakeside Building

The Riverside Press, Cambridge

The Riverside Press, Cambridge, Mass., U. S. A.
Electrotyped and Printed by H. O. Houghton & Company.

<u>Printing Statement:</u>

Due to the very old age and scarcity of this book,
many of the pages may be hard to read due to the
blurring of the original text, possible missing pages,
missing text, dark backgrounds and other issues
beyond our control.

Because this is such an important and rare work, we
believe it is best to reproduce this book regardless of
its original condition.

Thank you for your understanding.

PREFACE.

———•———

THE biographical sketch by Emerson which precedes the two papers by Thoreau, here printed, has this advantage over most biographies, that it helps one to understand the real man, and does not shut up the reader's interest in a knowledge of the mere circumstances of Thoreau's life. It is like a portrait which carries the eye straight to the character of the man portrayed, and does not arrest it at the dress or decorations. Indeed, Emerson was so impressed by the life and character of Thoreau that he forgot to mention the fact of his death. Thoreau died May 6, 1862. The only full narrative of his life is to be found in the volume *Henry D. Thoreau*, contributed by his friend and fellow-townsman, F. B. Sanborn, to the series of *American Men of Letters*.

Thoreau's own writings, however, furnish a still fuller account of his observations and thoughts. The first to appear was *A Week on the Concord and Merrimac Rivers*, published in 1849. It was a narrative of the adventure which he and his brother enjoyed ten years before, shortly after he graduated from college, when in a boat of their own making

they followed the Concord River to where it enter
the Merrimac, then went up that river to its source,
and finally back to the starting-place at Concord.
In 1845 he built a hut in the woods by Walden
Pond, where he lived for two years, watching the
life in woods and pond and air. *Walden*, published
in 1854, is his most famous book, and contains the
record of his experience as a hermit. These two
books were the only ones by Thoreau published in his
lifetime, but he contributed occasionally to periodi-
cals, and he kept full journals. After his death his
printed papers were gathered, and his journals drawn
from to make *Excursions in Field and Forest, The
Maine Woods, Cape Cod, Letters to Various Persons, A Yankee in Canada, Early Spring in Massachusetts*, and *Summer*. The two papers which follow, as well as Emerson's sketch, are from the volume
of *Excursions*.

CONTENTS.

BIOGRAPHICAL SKETCH OF THOREAU.

BY RALPH WALDO EMERSON.

HENRY DAVID THOREAU was the last male descendant of a French ancestor who came to this country from the Isle of Guernsey. His character exhibited occasional traits drawn from this blood, in singular combination with a very strong Saxon genius.

He was born in Concord, Massachusetts, on the 12th of July, 1817. He was graduated at Harvard College in 1837, but without any literary distinction. An iconoclast in literature, he seldom thanked colleges for their service to him, holding them in small esteem, whilst yet his debt to them was important. After leaving the University, he joined his brother in teaching a private school, which he soon renounced. His father was a manufacturer of lead-pencils, and Henry applied himself for a time to this craft, believing he could make a better pencil than was then in use. After completing his experiments, he exhibited his work to chemists and artists in Boston, and having obtained their certificates to its excellence and to its equality with the best London manufacture, he returned home contented. His friends congratulated him that he had now opened his way to fortune. But he replied, that he should never make another pencil. "Why should I? I would not do again what I have done once." He resumed his endless walks and miscellaneous studies, making every day some new acquaintance with Nature, though as yet never speaking of zoölogy or botany, since, though very studious of natural facts, he was incurious of technical and textual science.

At this time, a strong, healthy youth, fresh from college, whilst all his companions were choosing their profession, or eager to begin some lucrative employment, it was inevitable that his thoughts should be exercised on the same question, and it required rare decision to refuse all the accustomed paths, and keep his solitary freedom at the cost of disappointing the natural expectations of his family and friends: all the more difficult that he had a perfect probity, was exact in securing his own independence, and in holding every man to the like duty. But Thoreau never faltered. He was a born protestant. He declined to give up his large ambition of knowledge and action for any narrow craft or profession, aiming at a much more comprehensive calling, the art of living well. If he slighted and defined the opinions of others, it was only that he was more intent to reconcile his practice with his own belief. Never idle or self-indulgent, he preferred, when he wanted money, earning it by some piece of manual labor agreeable to him, as building a boat or a fence, planting, grafting, surveying, or other short work, to any long engagements. With his hardy habits and few wants, his skill in wood-craft, and his powerful arithmetic, he was very competent to live in any part of the world. It would cost him less time to supply his wants than another. He was therefore secure of his leisure.

A natural skill for mensuration, growing out of his

mathematical knowledge, and his habit of ascertaining the measures and distances of objects which interested him, the size of trees, the depth and extent of ponds and rivers, the height of mountains, and the air-line distance of his favorite summits, — this, and his intimate knowledge of the territory about Concord, made him drift into the profession of land-surveyor. It had the advantage for him that it led him continually into new and secluded grounds, and helped his studies of Nature. His accuracy and skill in this work were readily appreciated, and he found all the employment he wanted.

He could easily solve the problems of the surveyor, but he was daily beset with graver questions, which he manfully confronted. He interrogated every custom, and wished to settle all his practice on an ideal foundation. He was a protestant *à l'outrance*, and few lives contain so many renunciations. He was bred to no profession; he never married; he lived alone; he never went to church; he never voted; he refused to pay a tax to the state; he ate no flesh, he drank no wine, he never knew the use of tobacco; and, though a naturalist, he used neither trap nor gun. He chose — wisely, no doubt, for himself — to be the bachelor of thought and Nature. He had no talent for wealth, and knew how to be poor without the least hint of squalor or inelegance. Perhaps he fell into his way of living without forecasting it much, but approved it with later wisdom. "I am often reminded," he wrote in his journal, "that, if I had bestowed on me the wealth of Crœsus, my aims must be still the same and my means essentially the same." He had no temptations to fight against, — no appetites, no passions, no taste for elegant trifles. A fine house, dress, the manners and talk of highly cultivated people were all thrown away on him. He much preferred a good Indian, and considered these refinements as impediments to conversation, wishing to meet his companion on the simplest terms. He declined invitations to dinner-parties, because there each was in every one's way, and he could not meet the individuals to any purpose. "They make their pride," he said, "in making their dinner cost much; I make my pride in making my dinner cost little." When asked at table what dish he preferred, he answered, "The nearest." He did not like the taste of wine, and never had a vice in his life. He said, "I have a faint recollection of pleasure derived from smoking dried lily-stems before I was a man. I had commonly a supply of these. I have never smoked anything more noxious."

He chose to be rich by making his wants few, and supplying them himself. In his travels, he used the railroad only to get over so much country as was unimportant to the present purpose, walking hundreds of miles, avoiding taverns, buying a lodging in farmers' and fishermen's houses, as cheaper and more agreeable to him, and because there he could better find the men and the information he wanted.

There was somewhat military in his nature, not to be subdued, always manly and able, but rarely tender, as if he did not feel himself except in opposition. He wanted a fallacy to expose, a blunder to pillory, I may say required a little sense of victory, a roll of the drum, to call his powers into full exercise. It cost him nothing to say No; indeed, he found it much easier than to say Yes. It seemed as if his first instinct on hearing a proposition was to controvert it, so impatient was he of the limitations of our daily thought. This habit, of course, is a little chilling to the social affections; and though the companion would in the end acquit him of any malice or untruth, yet it mars conversation. Hence, no equal companion stood in affectionate relations with one so pure and guileless. " I love Henry," said one of his friends, " but I cannot like him; and as for taking his arm, I should as soon think of taking the arm of an elm-tree."

Yet, hermit and stoic as he was, he was really fond of sympathy, and threw himself heartily and childlike into the company of young people whom he loved, and whom he delighted to entertain, as he only could, with the varied and endless anecdotes of his experiences by field and river; and he was always ready to lead a huckleberry party or a search for chestnuts or grapes. Talking, one day, of a public discourse, Henry remarked, that whatever succeeded with the audience was bad. I said, "Who would not like to write something which all can read, like ' Robinson Crusoe '? and who does not see with regret that his page is not solid with a right materialistic treatment, which delights everybody?" Henry objected, of course, and vaunted the better lectures which reached only a few persons. But, at supper, a young girl, understanding that he was to lecture at the Lyceum, sharply asked him, " whether his lecture would be a nice, interesting story, such as she wished to hear, or whether it was one of those old philosophical things that she did not care about." Henry turned to her, and bethought himself, and, I saw, was trying to believe that he had matter that might fit her and her brother, who were to sit up and go to the lecture, if it was a good one for them.

He was a speaker and actor of the truth, born such, and was ever running into dramatic situations from this cause. In any circumstance, it interested all by-standers to know what part Henry would take, and what he would say; and he did not disappoint expectation, but used an original judgment on each emergency. In 1845 he built himself a small framed house on the shores of Walden Pond, and lived there two years alone, a life of labor and study. This action was quite native and fit for him. No one who knew him would tax him with affectation. He was more unlike his neighbors in his thought than in his action. As soon as he had exhausted the advantages of that solitude, he abandoned it. In 1847, not approving some uses to which the public expenditure was applied, he refused to pay his town tax, and was put in jail. A friend paid the tax for him, and he was released. The like annoyance was threatened the next year. But, as his friends paid the tax, notwithstanding his protest, I believe he ceased to resist. No opposition or ridicule had any weight with him. He coldly and fully stated his opinion without affecting to believe that it was the opinion of the company. It was of no consequence if every one present held the opposite opinion. On one occasion he went to the University Library to procure some books. The librarian refused to lend them. Mr. Thoreau repaired to the president, who stated to him the rules and usages which permitted the loan of books to resident graduates, to clergymen who were alumni, and to some others resident within a circle of ten miles' radius from the college. Mr. Thoreau explained to the president that the railroad had destroyed the old scale of distances, — that the library was useless, yes,

and President and College useless, on the terms of
his rules, — that the one benefit he owed to the College was its library, — that, at this moment, not only
his want of books was imperative, but he wanted a
large number of books, and assured him that he,
Thoreau, and not the librarian, was the proper custo-
dian of these. In short, the President found the peti-
tioner so formidable, and the rules getting to look so
ridiculous, that he ended by giving him a privilege
which in his hands proved unlimited thereafter.

No truer American existed than Thoreau. His
preference of his country and condition was genuine,
and his aversation from English and European manners and tastes almost reached contempt. He listened
impatiently to news or *bon mots* gleaned from London
circles; and though he tried to be civil, these anecdotes fatigued him. The men were all imitating each
other, and on a small mould. Why can they not live
as far apart as possible, and each be a man by himself? What he sought was the most energetic nature; and he wished to go to Oregon, not to London.
"In every part of Great Britain," he wrote in his
diary, "are discovered traces of the Romans, their
funereal urns, their camps, their roads, their dwellings.
But New England, at least, is not based on any Roman ruins. We have not to lay the foundations of
our houses on the ashes of a former civilization."

But, idealist as he was, standing for abolition of
slavery, abolition of tariffs, almost for abolition of
government, it is needless to say he found himself
not only unrepresented in actual politics, but almost
equally opposed to every class of reformers. Yet he
paid the tribute of his uniform respect to the Anti-
Slavery Party. One man, whose personal acquaint-

ance he had formed, he honored with exceptional regard.   Before the first friendly word had been spoken
for Captain John Brown, after the arrest, he sent no-
tices to most houses in Concord, that he would speak
in a public hall on the condition and character of
John Brown, on Sunday evening, and invited all to
come.   The Republican Committee, the Abolitionist
Committee, sent him word that it was premature and
not advisable.   He replied, " I did not send to you
for advice, but to announce that I am to speak."   The
hall was filled at an early hour by people of all parties, and his earnest eulogy of the hero was heard by
all respectfully, by many with a sympathy that surprised themselves.

It was said of Plotinus that he was ashamed of his
body, and 't is very likely he had good reason for it,
— that his body was a bad servant, and he had not
skill in dealing with the material world, as happens
often to men of abstract intellect.   But Mr. Thoreau
was equipped with a most adapted and serviceable
body.   He was of short stature, firmly built, of light
complexion, with strong, serious blue eyes, and a
grave aspect, — his face covered in the late years with
a becoming beard.   His senses were acute, his frame
well-knit and hardy, his hands strong and skilful in
the use of tools.   And there was a wonderful fitness
of body and mind.   He could pace sixteen rods more
accurately than another man could measure them with
rod and chain.   He could find his path in the woods
at night, he said, better by his feet than his eyes.
He could estimate the measure of a tree very well by
his eye; he could estimate the weight of a calf or a
pig, like a dealer.   From a box containing a bushel
or more of loose pencils, he could take up with his

hands fast enough just a dozen pencils at every grasp. He was a good swimmer, runner, skater, boatman, and would probably outwalk most countrymen in a day's journey. And the relation of body to mind was still finer than we have indicated. He said he wanted every stride his legs made. The length of his walk uniformly made the length of his writing. If shut up in the house, he did not write at all.

He had a strong common sense, like that which Rose Flammock, the weaver's daughter, in Scott's romance, commends in her father, as resembling a yardstick, which, whilst it measures dowlas and diaper, can equally well measure tapestry and cloth of gold. He had always a new resource. When I was planting forest-trees, and had procured half a peck of acorns, he said that only a small portion of them would be sound, and proceeded to examine them, and select the sound ones. But finding this took time, he said, " I think, if you put them all into water, the good ones will sink; " which experiment we tried with success. He could plan a garden, or a house, or a barn ; would have been competent to lead a " Pacific Exploring Expedition " ; could give judicious counsel in the gravest private or public affairs.

He lived for the day, not cumbered and mortified by his memory. If he brought you yesterday a new proposition, he would bring you to-day another not less revolutionary. A very industrious man, and setting, like all highly organized men, a high value on his time, he seemed the only man of leisure in town, always ready for any excursion that promised well, or for conversation prolonged into late hours. His trenchant sense was never stopped by his rules of daily prudence, but was always up to the new occasion.

He liked and used the simplest food, yet, when some one urged a vegetable diet, Thoreau thought all diets a very small matter, saying that "the man who shoots the buffalo lives better than the man who boards at the Graham House." He said, — "You can sleep near the railroad, and never be disturbed: Nature knows very well what sounds are worth attending to, and has made up her mind not to hear the railroad-whistle. But things respect the devout mind, and a mental ecstasy was never interrupted." He noted what repeatedly befell him, that, after receiving from a distance a rare plant, he would presently find the same in his own haunts. And those pieces of luck which happen only to good players happened to him. One day, walking with a stranger, who inquired where Indian arrow-heads could be found, he replied, " Everywhere," and, stooping forward, picked one on the instant from the ground. At Mount Washington, in Tuckerman's Ravine, Thoreau had a bad fall, and sprained his foot. As he was in the act of getting up from his fall, he saw for the first time the leaves of the *Arnica mollis.*[1]

His robust common sense, armed with stout hands, keen perceptions, and strong will, cannot yet account for the superiority which shone in his simple and hidden life. I must add the cardinal fact, that there was an excellent wisdom in him, proper to a rare class of men, which showed him the material world as a means and symbol. This discovery, which sometimes yields to poets a certain casual and interrupted light, serving for the ornament of their writing, was in him

[1] A plant with healing virtue, found in the mountains of New Hampshire and New York, and also about Lake Superior.

an unsleeping insight; and whatever faults or ob-
structions of temperament might cloud it, he was not
disobedient to the heavenly vision.   In his youth, he
said, one day, " The other world is all my art: my
pencils will draw no other; my jack-knife will cut
nothing else; I do not use it as a means." This was
the muse and genius that ruled his opinions, conversation, studies, work, and course of life.   This made
him a searching judge of men.   At first glance he
measured his companion, and, though insensible to
some fine traits of culture, could very well report his
weight and calibre.   And this made the impression
of genius which his conversation sometimes gave.

He understood the matter in hand at a glance, and
saw the limitations and poverty of those he talked
with, so that nothing seemed concealed from such terrible eyes.   I have repeatedly known young men of
sensibility converted in a moment to the belief that
this was the man they were in search of, the man
of men, who could tell them all they should do.   His
own dealing with them was never affectionate, but
superior, didactic, scorning their petty ways, — very
slowly conceding, or not conceding at all, the prom-
ise of his society at their houses, or even at his
own.   " Would he not walk with them ? "   " He
did not know.   There was nothing so important to
him as his walk; he had no walks to throw away
on company."   Visits were offered him from respect-
ful parties, but he declined them.   Admiring friends
offered to carry him at their own cost to the Yel-
lowstone River, — to the West Indies, — to South
America.   But though nothing could be more grave
or considered than his refusals, they remind one in
quite new relations of that fop Brummel's reply to

the gentleman who offered him his carriage in a shower, " But where will *you* ride, then ? " — and what accusing silences, and what searching and irresistible speeches, battering down all defences, his companions can remember.

Mr. Thoreau dedicated his genius with such entire love to the fields, hills, and waters of his native town, that he made them known and interesting to all reading Americans, and to people over the sea. The river on whose banks he was born and died he knew from its springs to its confluence with the Merrimack. He had made summer and winter observations on it for many years, and at every hour of the day and night. The result of the recent survey of the Water Commissioners appointed by the State of Massachusetts he had reached by his private experiments, several years earlier. Every fact which occurs in the bed, on the banks, or in the air over it; the fishes, and their spawning and nests, their manners, their food; the shad-flies which fill the air on a certain evening once a year, and which are snapped at by the fishes so ravenously that many of these die of repletion; the conical heaps of small stones on the river-shallows, one of which heaps will sometimes overfill a cart, — these heaps the huge nests of small fishes; the birds which frequent the stream, heron, duck, sheldrake, loon, osprey; the snake, musk-rat, otter, woodchuck, and fox, on the banks; the turtle, frog, hyla, and cricket, which make the banks vocal, — were well known to him, and, as it were, townsmen and fellow-creatures; so that he felt an absurdity or violence in any narrative of one of these by itself apart, and still more of its dimensions on an inch-rule, or in the exhibition of its skeleton, or the specimen of a squirrel or a bird in brandy. He liked to speak of the manners of the river, as itself a lawful creature, yet with exactness, and always to an observed fact. As he knew the river, so the ponds in this region.

One of the weapons he used, more important than microscope or alcohol-receiver to other investigators, was a whim which grew on him by indulgence, yet appeared in gravest statement, namely, of extolling his own town and neighborhood as the most favored centre for natural observation. He remarked that the flora of Massachusetts embraced almost all the important plants of America, — most of the oaks, most of the willows, the best pines, the ash, the maple, the beech, the nuts. He returned Kane's "Arctic Voyage" to a friend of whom he had borrowed it, with the remark that "most of the phenomena noted might be observed in Concord." He seemed a little envious of the Pole, for the coincident sunrise and sunset, or five minutes' day after six months : a splendid fact, which Annursnuc[1] had never afforded him. He found red snow in one of his walks, and told me that he expected to find yet the *Victoria regia* in Concord. He was the attorney of the indigenous plants, and owned to a preference of the weeds to the imported plants, as of the Indian to the civilized man ; and noticed with pleasure that the willow bean-poles of his neighbor had grown more than his beans. " See these weeds," he said, " which have been hoed at by a million farmers all spring and summer, and yet have prevailed, and just now come out triumphant over all lanes, pastures, fields, and gardens, such is their vigor. We have insulted them with low names, too, — as Pigweed, Wormwood, Chickweed, Shad-Blossom." He

[1] A hill in Concord on the border of Acton.

says, "They have brave names, too, — Ambrosia, Stellaria, Amelanchier, Amaranth, etc."

I think his fancy for referring everything to the meridian of Concord did not grow out of any ignorance or depreciation of other longitudes or latitudes, but was rather a playful expression of his conviction of the indifferency of all places, and that the best place for each is where he stands. He expressed it once in this wise: "I think nothing is to be hoped from you, if this bit of mould under your feet is not sweeter to you to eat than any other in this world, or in any world."

The other weapon with which he conquered all obstacles in science was patience. He knew how to sit immovable — a part of the rock he rested on — until the bird, the reptile, the fish, which had retired from him, should come back and resume its habits, — nay, moved by curiosity, should come to him and watch him.

It was a pleasure and a privilege to walk with him. He knew the country like a fox or a bird, and passed through it as freely by paths of his own. He knew every track in the snow or on the ground, and what creature had taken this path before him. One must submit abjectly to such a guide, and the reward was great. Under his arm he carried an old music-book to press plants; in his pocket, his diary and pencil, a spy-glass for birds, microscope, jack-knife, and twine. He wore straw hat, stout shoes, strong gray trousers to brave shrub-oaks and smilax, and to climb a tree for a hawk's or a squirrel's nest. He waded into the pool for the water-plants, and his strong legs were no insignificant part of his armor. On the day I speak of he looked for the Menyanthes, detected it across the wide pool, and, on examination of the florets, decided that it had been in flower five days. He drew out of his breast-pocket his diary, and read the names of all the plants that should bloom on this day, whereof he kept account as a banker when his notes fall due. The Cypripedium not due till to-morrow. He thought that, if he waked up from a trance in this swamp, he could tell by the plants what time of the year it was within two days. The redstart was flying about, and presently the fine grosbeaks, whose brilliant scarlet makes "the rash gazer wipe his eye,"[1] and whose fine clear note Thoreau compared to that of a tanager which has got rid of its hoarseness. Presently he heard a note which he called that of the night-warbler, a bird he had never identified, had been in search of twelve years, which always, when he saw it, was in the act of diving down into a tree or bush, and which it was vain to seek; the only bird which sings indifferently by night and by day. I told him he must beware of finding and booking it, lest life should have nothing more to show him. He said, " What you seek in vain for, half your life, one day you come full upon, — all the family at dinner. You seek it like a dream, and as soon as you find it you become its prey."

His interest in the flower or the bird lay very deep in his mind, — was connected with Nature, — and the meaning of Nature was never attempted to be defined by him. He would not offer a memoir of his observa-

---

[1] Sweet Rose! whose hue, angry and brave,
   Bids the rash gazer wipe his eye :
   Thy root is ever in its grave, —
      And thou must die.
            Virtue : GEORGE HERBERT.

tions to the Natural History Society. "Why should
I? To detach the description from its connections
in my mind would make it no longer true or valuable
to me; and they do not wish what belongs to it."
His power of observation seemed to indicate additional senses. He saw as with microscope, heard as
with ear-trumpet, and his memory was a photographic
register of all he saw and heard. And yet none knew
better than he that it is not the fact that imports, but
the impression or effect of the fact on your mind.
Every fact lay in glory in his mind, a type of the
order and beauty of the whole.

His determination on Natural History was organic.
He confessed that he sometimes felt like a hound or a
panther, and, if born among Indians, would have been
a fell hunter. But, restrained by his Massachusetts
culture, he played out the game in this mild form of
botany and ichthyology. His intimacy with animals
suggested what Thomas Fuller records of Butler the
apiologist, that "either he had told the bees things
or the bees had told him." Snakes coiled round his
leg; the fishes swam into his hand, and he took them
out of the water; he pulled the woodchuck out of its
hole by the tail, and took the foxes under his protec-
tion from the hunters. Our naturalist had perfect
magnanimity; he had no secrets: he would carry you
to the heron's haunt, or even to his most prized botanical swamp, — possibly knowing that you could
never find it again, yet willing to take his risks.

No college ever offered him a diploma, or a profes-
sor's chair; no academy made him its corresponding
secretary, its discoverer, or even its member. Perhaps these learned bodies feared the satire of his
presence. Yet so much knowledge of Nature's secret

and genius few others possessed, none in a more large and religious synthesis. For not a particle of respect had he to the opinions of any man or body of men, but homage solely to the truth itself; and as he discovered everywhere among doctors some leaning of courtesy, it discredited them. He grew to be revered and admired by his townsmen, who had at first known him only as an oddity. The farmers who employed him as a surveyor soon discovered his rare accuracy and skill, his knowledge of their lands, of trees, of birds, of Indian remains and the like, which enabled him to tell every farmer more than he knew before of his own farm; so that he began to feel a little as if Mr. Thoreau had better rights in his land than he. They felt, too, the superiority of character which addressed all men with a native authority.

Indian relics abound in Concord, — arrow-heads, stone chisels, pestles, and fragments of pottery; and on the river-bank, large heaps of clam-shells and ashes mark spots which the savages frequented. These, and every circumstance touching the Indian, were important in his eyes. His visits to Maine were chiefly for love of the Indian. He had the satisfaction of seeing the manufacture of the bark-canoe, as well as of trying his hand in its management on the rapids. He was inquisitive about the making of the stone arrow-head, and in his last days charged a youth setting out for the Rocky Mountains to find an Indian who could tell him that: "It was well worth a visit to California to learn it." Occasionally, a small party of Penobscot Indians would visit Concord, and pitch their tents for a few weeks in summer on the river-bank. He failed not to make acquaintance with the best of them; though he well knew that asking questions of Indians is like catechizing beavers and rabbits. In his last visit to Maine he had great satisfaction from Joseph Polis, an intelligent Indian of Oldtown, who was his guide for some weeks.

He was equally interested in every natural fact. The depth of his perception found likeness of law throughout Nature, and I know not any genius who so swiftly inferred universal law from the single fact. He was no pedant of a department. His eye was open to beauty, and his ear to music. He found these, not in rare conditions, but wheresoever he went. He thought the best of music was in single strains; and he found poetic suggestion in the humming of the telegraph wire.

His poetry might be bad or good; he no doubt wanted a lyric facility and technical skill; but he had the source of poetry in his spiritual perception. He was a good reader and critic, and his judgment on poetry was to the ground of it. He could not be deceived as to the presence or absence of the poetic element in any composition, and his thirst for this made him negligent and perhaps scornful of superficial graces. He would pass by many delicate rhythms, but he would have detected every live stanza or line in a volume, and knew very well where to find an equal poetic charm in prose. He was so enamored of the spiritual beauty that he held all actual written poems in very light esteem in the comparison. He admired Æschylus and Pindar; but, when some one was commending them, he said that Æschylus and the Greeks, in describing Apollo and Orpheus, had given no song, or no good one. "They ought not to have moved trees, but to have chanted to the gods such a hymn as would have sung all their old ideas out of

their heads, and new ones in." His own verses are
often rude and defective. The gold does not yet run
pure, — is drossy and crude. The thyme and mar-
joram are not yet honey. But if he want lyric fine-
ness and technical merits, if he have not the poetic
temperament, he never lacks the causal thought, show-
ing that his genius was better than his talent. He
knew the worth of the Imagination for the uplifting
and consolation of human life, and liked to throw
every thought into a symbol. The fact you tell is of
no value, but only the impression. For this reason
his presence was poetic, always piqued the curiosity
to know more deeply the secrets of his mind. He
had many reserves, an unwillingness to exhibit to pro-
fane eyes what was still sacred in his own, and knew
well how to throw a poetic veil over his experience.
All readers of " Walden" will remember his myth-
ical record of his disappointments: —

" I long ago lost a hound, a bay horse, and a turtle-
dove, and am still on their trail. Many are the trav-
ellers I have spoken concerning them, describing their
tracks, and what calls they answered to. I have met
one or two who had heard the hound, and the tramp
of the horse, and even seen the dove disappear behind
a cloud; and they seemed as anxious to recover them
as if they had lost them themselves." [1]

His riddles were worth the reading, and I confide,
that, if at any time I do not understand the expression,
it is yet just. Such was the wealth of his truth that it
was not worth his while to use words in vain. His
poem entitled " Sympathy" reveals the tenderness
under that triple steel of stoicism, and the intellec-
tual subtilty it could animate. His classic poem on

[1] *Walden*, p. 20.

" Smoke " suggests Simonides, but is better than any poem of Simonides. His biography is in his verses. His habitual thought makes all his poetry a hymn to the Cause of causes, the Spirit which vivifies and controls his own.

> "I hearing get, who had but ears,
>   And sight, who had but eyes before ;
> I moments live, who lived but years,
>   And truth discern, who knew but learning's lore."

And still more in these religious lines : —

> " Now chiefly is my natal hour,
>   And only now my prime of life ;
> I will not doubt the love untold,
> Which not my worth or want have bought,
> Which wooed me young, and wooes me old,
> And to this evening hath me brought."

Whilst he used in his writings a certain petulance of remark in reference to churches or churchmen, he was a person of a rare, tender, and absolute religion, a person incapable of any profanation, by act or by thought. Of course, the same isolation which belonged to his original thinking and living detached him from the social religious forms. This is neither to be censured nor regretted. Aristotle long ago explained it, when he said, " One who surpasses his fellow-citizens in virtue is no longer a part of the city. Their law is not for him, since he is a law to himself."

Thoreau was sincerity itself, and might fortify the convictions of prophets in the ethical laws by his holy living. It was an affirmative experience which refused to be set aside. A truth-speaker he, capable of the most deep and strict conversation ; a physician to the wounds of any soul ; a friend, knowing not only the secret of friendship, but almost worshipped by those few persons who resorted to him as their confessor and prophet, and knew the deep value of his mind and great heart. He thought that without religion or devotion of some kind nothing great was ever accomplished : and he thought that the bigoted sectarian had better bear this in mind.

His virtues, of course, sometimes ran into extremes. It was easy to trace to the inexorable demand on all for exact truth that austerity which made this willing hermit more solitary even than he wished. Himself of a perfect probity, he required not less of others. He had a disgust at crime, and no worldly success could cover it. He detected paltering as readily in dignified and prosperous persons as in beggars, and with equal scorn. Such dangerous frankness was in his dealing that his admirers called him "that terrible Thoreau," as if he spoke when silent, and was still present when he had departed. I think the severity of his ideal interfered to deprive him of a healthy sufficiency of human society.

The habit of a realist to find things the reverse of their appearance inclined him to put every statement in a paradox. A certain habit of antagonism defaced his earlier writings, — a trick of rhetoric not quite outgrown in his later, of substituting for the obvious word and thought its diametrical opposite. He praised wild mountains and winter forests for their domestic air, in snow and ice he would find sultriness, and commended the wilderness for resembling Rome and Paris. "It was so dry, that you might call it wet."

The tendency to magnify the moment, to read all the laws of Nature in the one object or one combination under your eye, is of course comic to those who do not share the philosopher's perception of identity. To him there was no such thing as size. The pond was a small ocean; the Atlantic, a large Walden Pond. He referred every minute fact to cosmical laws. Though he meant to be just, he seemed haunted by a certain chronic assumption that the science of the day pretended completeness, and he had just found out that the *savans* had neglected to discriminate a particular botanical variety, had failed to describe the seeds or count the sepals. "That is to say," he replied, "the blockheads were not born in Concord; but who said they were? It was their unspeakable misfortune to be born in London, or Paris, or Rome; but, poor fellows, they did what they could, considering that they never saw Bateman's Pond, or Nine-Acre Corner, or Becky-Stow's Swamp. Besides, what were you sent into the world for, but to add this observation?"

Had his genius been only contemplative, he had been fitted to his life, but with his energy and practical ability he seemed born for great enterprise and for command; and I so much regret the loss of his rare powers of action, that I cannot help counting it a fault in him that he had no ambition. Wanting this, instead of engineering for all America, he was the captain of a huckleberry party. Pounding beans is good to the end of pounding empires one of these days; but if, at the end of years, it is still only beans!

But these foibles, real or apparent, were fast vanishing in the incessant growth of a spirit so robust and wise, and which effaced its defeats with new triumphs. His study of Nature was a perpetual ornament to him, and inspired his friends with curiosity to see the world through his eyes, and to hear his adventures. They possessed every kind of interest.

He had many elegancies of his own, whilst he scoffed at conventional elegance. Thus, he could not bear to hear the sound of his own steps, the grit of gravel; and therefore never willingly walked in the road, but in the grass, on mountains and in woods. His senses were acute, and he remarked that by night every dwelling-house gives out bad air, like a slaughter-house. He liked the pure fragrance of melilot.[1] He honored certain plants with special regard, and, over all, the pond-lily,— then, the gentian, and the *Mikania scandens*,[2] and "life-everlasting," and a bass - tree which he visited every year when it bloomed, in the middle of July. He thought the scent a more oracular inquisition than the sight, — more oracular and trustworthy. The scent, of course, reveals what is concealed from the other senses. By it he detected earthiness. He delighted in echoes, and said they were almost the only kind of kindred voices that he heard. He loved Nature so well, was so happy in her solitude, that he became very jealous of cities, and the sad work which their refinements and artifices made with man and his dwelling. The axe was always destroying his forest. "Thank God," he said, "they cannot cut down the clouds!" "All kinds of figures are drawn on the blue ground with this fibrous white paint."

I subjoin a few sentences taken from his unpublished manuscripts, not only as records of his thought and feeling, but for their power of description and literary excellence.

[1] Sweet clover.   [2] Climbing hemp-weed.

"Some circumstantial evidence is very strong, as when you find a trout in the milk."

"The chub is a soft fish, and tastes like boiled brown paper salted."

"The youth gets together his materials to build a bridge to the moon, or, perchance, a palace or temple on the earth, and at length the middle-aged man concludes to build a wood-shed with them."

"The locust z-ing."

"Devil's-needles zigzagging along the Nut-Meadow brook."

"Sugar is not so sweet to the palate as sound to the healthy ear."

"I put on some hemlock-boughs, and the rich salt crackling of their leaves was like mustard to the ear, the crackling of uncountable regiments. Dead trees love the fire."

"The bluebird carries the sky on his back."

"The tanager flies through the green foliage as if it would ignite the leaves."

"If I wish for a horse-hair for my compass-sight, I must go to the stable; but the hair-bird, with her sharp eyes, goes to the road."

"Immortal water, alive even to the superficies."

"Fire is the most tolerable third party."

"Nature made ferns for pure leaves, to show what she could do in that line."

"No tree has so fair a bole and so handsome an instep as the beech."

"How did these beautiful rainbow-tints get into the shell of the fresh-water clam, buried in the mud at the bottom of our dark river?"

"Hard are the times when the infant's shoes are second-foot."

"We are strictly confined to our men to whom we give liberty."

"Of what significance the things you can forget? A little thought is sexton to all the world."

"How can we expect a harvest of thought who have not had a seed-time of character?"

"Only he can be trusted with gifts who can present a face of bronze to expectations."

"I ask to be melted. You can only ask of the metals that they be tender to the fire that melts them. To naught else can they be tender."

There is a flower known to botanists, one of the same genus with our summer plant called "Life Everlasting," a *Gnaphalium* like that, which grows on the most inaccessible cliffs of the Tyrolese mountains, where the chamois dare hardly venture, and which the hunter, tempted by its beauty, and by his love, (for it is immensely valued by the Swiss maidens,) climbs the cliffs to gather, and is sometimes found dead at the foot, with the flower in his hand. It is called by botanists the *Gnaphalium leontopodium*, but by the Swiss *Edelweiss*,[1] which signifies *Noble Purity*. Thoreau seemed to me living in the hope to gather this plant, which belonged to him of right. The scale on which his studies proceeded was so large as to require longevity, and we were the less prepared for his sudden disappearance. The country knows not yet, or in the least part, how great a son it has lost. It seems an injury that he should leave in the midst his broken task, which none else can finish, — a kind of indignity to so noble a soul, that he should depart out of Nature before yet he has been

---

[1] Pronounced *ā'del-vice.*

really shown to his peers for what he is. But he, at least, is content. His soul was made for the noblest society; he had in a short life exhausted the capabilities of this world; wherever there is knowledge, wherever there is virtue, wherever there is beauty, he will find a home.

THE SUCCESSION OF FOREST TREES.

EVERY man is entitled to come to Cattle-show, even a transcendentalist;[1] and for my part I am more interested in the men than in the cattle. I wish to see once more those old familiar faces, whose names I do not know, which for me represent the Middlesex[2] country, and come as near being indigenous to the soil as a white man can; the men who are not above their business, whose coats are not too black, whose shoes do not shine very much, who never wear gloves to conceal their hands. It is true, there are some queer specimens of humanity attracted to our festival, but all are welcome. I am pretty sure to meet once more that weak-minded and whimsical fellow, generally weak-bodied too, who prefers a crooked stick for a cane; perfectly useless, you would say, only bizarre, fit for a cabinet, like a petrified snake. A ram's horn would be as convenient, and is yet more curiously twisted. He brings that much indulged bit of the country with him, from some town's end or other, and introduces it to Concord groves, as if he had promised it so much sometime. So some, it seems

[1] The name transcendentalist was given to Emerson, Thoreau, and others of similar ways of thinking.

[2] Concord is in Middlesex County, Massachusetts, and this paper was an address read to the Middlesex Agricultural Society at the fair commonly called a Cattle-show.

to me, elect their rulers for their crookedness.   But I think that a straight stick makes the best cane, and an upright man the best ruler.   Or why choose a man to do plain work who is distinguished for his oddity ?   However, I do not know but you will think that they have committed this mistake who invited me to speak to you to-day.

In my capacity of surveyor I have often talked with some of you, my employers, at your dinner-tables, after having gone round and round and behind your farming, and ascertained exactly what its limits were. Moreover, taking a surveyor's and a naturalist's liberty, I have been in the habit of going across your lots much oftener than is usual, as many of you, perhaps to your sorrow, are aware.   Yet many of you, to my relief, have seemed not to be aware of it; and when I came across you in some out-of-the-way nook of your farms, have inquired, with an air of surprise, if I were not lost, since you had never seen me in that part of the town or county before ; when, if the truth were known, and it had not been for betraying my secret, I might with more propriety have inquired if *you* were not lost, since I had never seen *you* there before.   I have several times shown the proprietor the shortest way out of his wood-lot.

Therefore, it would seem that I have some title to speak to you to-day ; and considering what that title is, and the occasion that has called us together, I need offer no apology if I invite your attention, for the few moments that are allotted me, to a purely scientific subject.

At those dinner-tables referred to, I have often been asked, as many of you have been, if I could tell how it happened, that when a pine wood was cut down an oak one commonly sprang up, and *vice versa*. To which I have answered, and now answer, that I can tell, — that it is no mystery to me. As I am not aware that this has been clearly shown by any one, I shall lay the more stress on this point. Let me lead you back into your wood-lots again.

When, hereabouts, a single forest tree or a forest springs up naturally where none of its kind grew before, I do not hesitate to say, though in some quarters still it may sound paradoxical, that it came from a seed. Of the various ways by which trees are *known* to be propagated, — by transplanting, cuttings, and the like, — this is the only supposable one under these circumstances. No such tree has ever been known to spring from anything else. If any one asserts that it sprang from something else, or from nothing, the burden of proof lies with him.

It remains, then, only to show how the seed is transported from where it grows to where it is planted. This is done chiefly by the agency of the wind, water, and animals. The lighter seeds, as those of pines and maples, are transported chiefly by wind and water ; the heavier, as acorns and nuts, by animals.

In all the pines, a very thin membrane, in appearance much like an insect's wing, grows over and around the seed, and independent of it, while the latter is being developed within its base. Indeed, this is often perfectly developed, though the seed is abortive ; nature being, you would say, more sure to provide the means of transporting the seed than to provide the seed to be transported. In other words, a beautiful thin sack is woven around the seed, with a handle to it such as the wind can take hold of, and it is then committed to the wind, expressly that it may transport the seed and extend the range of the species; and this it does as effectually as when seeds are sent by mail in a different kind of sack from the patent-office. There is a patent-office at the seat of government of the universe, whose managers are as much interested in the dispersion of seeds as anybody at Washington can be, and their operations are infinitely more extensive and regular.

There is then no necessity for supposing that the pines have sprung up from nothing, and I am aware that I am not at all peculiar in asserting that they come from seeds, though the mode of their propagation *by nature* has been but little attended to. They are very extensively raised from the seed in Europe, and are beginning to be here.

When you cut down an oak wood, a pine wood will not *at once* spring up there unless there are, or have been, quite recently, seed-bearing pines near enough for the seeds to be blown from them. But, adjacent to a forest of pines, if you prevent other crops from growing there, you will surely have an extension of your pine forest, provided the soil is suitable.

As for the heavy seeds and nuts which are not furnished with wings, the notion is still a very common one that, when the trees which bear these spring up where none of their kind were noticed before, they have come from seeds or other principles spontaneously generated there in an unusual manner, or which have lain dormant in the soil for centuries, or perhaps been called into activity by the heat of a burning. I do not believe these assertions, and I will state some of the ways in which, according to my observation, such forests are planted and raised.

Every one of these seeds, too, will be found to be
winged or legged in another fashion. Surely it is not
wonderful that cherry-trees of all kinds are widely
dispersed, since their fruit is well known to be the
favorite food of various birds. Many kinds are called
bird-cherries, and they appropriate many more kinds,
which are not so called. Eating cherries is a bird-
like employment, and unless we disperse the seeds
occasionally, as they do, I shall think that the birds
have the best right to them. See how artfully the
seed of a cherry is placed in order that a bird may be
compelled to transport it — in the very midst of a
tempting pericarp, so that the creature that would de-
vour this must commonly take the stone also into its
mouth or bill. If you ever ate a cherry and did not
make two bites of it, you must have perceived it —
right in the centre of the luscious morsel, a large
earthy residuum left on the tongue. We thus take
into our mouths cherry-stones as big as peas, a dozen
at once, for Nature can persuade us to do almost
anything when she would compass her ends. Some
wild men and children instinctively swallow these, as
the birds do when in a hurry, it being the shortest
way to get rid of them. Thus, though these seeds
are not provided with vegetable wings, Nature has
impelled the thrush tribe to take them into their
bills and fly away with them; and they are winged
in another sense, and more effectually than the seeds
of pines, for these are carried even against the wind.
The consequence is, that cherry-trees grow not only
here but there. The same is true of a great many
other seeds.

But to come to the observation which suggested
these remarks. As I have said, I suspect that I can

throw some light on the fact, that when hereabouts a
dense pine wood is cut down, oaks and other hard
woods may at once take its place. I have got only to
show that the acorns and nuts, provided they are
grown in the neighborhood, are regularly planted in
such woods ; for I assert that if an oak-tree has not
grown within ten miles, and man has not carried
acorns thither, then an oak wood will not spring up
at once, when a pine wood is cut down.

Apparently, there were only pines there before.
They are cut off, and after a year or two you see oaks
and other hard woods springing up there, with scarcely
a pine amid them, and the wonder commonly is, how
the seed could have lain in the ground so long without decaying. But the truth is, that it has not lain in
the ground so long, but is regularly planted each year
by various quadrupeds and birds.

In this neighborhood, where oaks and pines are
about equally dispersed, if you look through the thick-
est pine wood, even the seemingly unmixed pitch-pine
ones, you will commonly detect many little .oaks,
birches, and other hard woods, sprung from seeds carried into the thicket by squirrels and other animals,
and also blown thither, but which are overshadowed
and choked by the pines. The denser the evergreen
wood, the more likely it is to be well planted with
these seeds, because the planters incline to resort
with their forage to the closest covert. They also
carry it into birch and other woods. This planting
is carried on annually, and the oldest seedlings annually die ; but when the pines are cleared off, the
oaks, having got just the start they want, and now
secured favorable conditions, immediately spring up
to trees.

The shade of a dense pine wood is more unfavorable to the springing up of pines of the same species than of oaks within it, though the former may come up abundantly when the pines are cut, if there chance to be sound seed in the ground.

But when you cut off a lot of hard wood, very often the little pines mixed with it have a similar start, for the squirrels have carried off the nuts to the pines, and not to the more open wood, and they commonly make pretty clean work of it; and moreover, if the wood was old, the sprouts will be feeble or entirely fail; to say nothing about the soil being, in a measure, exhausted for this kind of crop.

If a pine wood is surrounded by a white-oak one chiefly, white-oaks may be expected to succeed when the pines are cut. If it is surrounded instead by an edging of shrub-oaks, then you will probably have a dense shrub-oak thicket.

I have no time to go into details, but will say, in a word, that while the wind is conveying the seeds of pines into hard woods and open lands, the squirrels and other animals are conveying the seeds of oaks and walnuts into the pine woods, and thus a rotation of crops is kept up.

I affirmed this confidently many years ago, and an occasional examination of dense pine woods confirmed me in my opinion. It has long been known to observers that squirrels bury nuts in the ground, but I am not aware that any one has thus accounted for the regular succession of forests.

On the 24th of September, in 1857, as I was paddling down the Assabet, in this town, I saw a red squirrel run along the bank under some herbage, with something large in its mouth. It stopped near the foot of a hemlock, within a couple of rods of me, and, hastily pawing a hole with its forefeet, dropped its booty into it, covered it up, and retreated part way up the trunk of the tree. As I approached the shore to examine the deposit, the squirrel, descending part way, betrayed no little anxiety about its treasure, and made two or three motions to recover it before it finally retreated. Digging there, I found two green pig-nuts joined together, with the thick husks on, buried about an inch and a half under the reddish soil of decayed hemlock leaves, — just the right depth to plant it. In short, this squirrel was then engaged in accomplishing two objects, to wit, laying up a store of winter food for itself, and planting a hickory wood for all creation. If the squirrel was killed, or neglected its deposit, a hickory would spring up. The nearest hickory tree was twenty rods distant. These nuts were there still just fourteen days later, but were gone when I looked again, November 21, or six weeks later still.

I have since examined more carefully several dense woods, which are said to be, and are apparently exclusively pine, and always with the same result. For instance, I walked the same day to a small but very dense and handsome white-pine grove, about fifteen rods square, in the east part of this town. The trees are large for Concord, being from ten to twenty inches in diameter, and as exclusively pine as any wood that I know. Indeed, I selected this wood because I thought it the least likely to contain anything else. It stands on an open plain or pasture, except that it adjoins another small pine wood, which has a few little oaks in it, on the southeast side. On every other side it was at least thirty rods from the nearest woods. Standing on the edge of this grove and looking through it, for it is quite level and free from underwood, for the most part bare, red-carpeted ground, you would have said that there was not a hard-wood tree in it, young or old. But on looking carefully along over its floor I discovered, though it was not till my eye had got used to the search, that, alternating with thin ferns and small blueberry bushes, there was, not merely here and there, but as often as every five feet and with a degree of regularity, a little oak, from three to twelve inches high, and in one place I found a green acorn dropped by the base of a pine.

I confess, I was surprised to find my theory so perfectly proved in this case. One of the principal agents in this planting, the red squirrels, were all the while curiously inspecting me, while I was inspecting their plantation. Some of the little oaks had been browsed by cows, which resorted to this wood for shade.

After seven or eight years, the hard woods evidently find such a locality unfavorable to their growth, the pines being allowed to stand. As an evidence of this, I observed a diseased red-maple twenty-five feet long, which had been recently prostrated, though it was still covered with green leaves, the only maple in any position in the wood.

But although these oaks almost invariably die if the pines are not cut down, it is probable that they do better for a few years under their shelter than they would anywhere else.

The very extensive and thorough experiments of the English have at length led them to adopt a method of raising oaks almost precisely like this, which somewhat earlier had been adopted by nature and her

squirrels here; they have simply rediscovered the
value of pines as nurses for oaks. The English ex-
perimenters seem early and generally to have found
out the importance of using trees of some kind as
nurse-plants for the young oaks. I quote from Loudon what he describes as " the ultimatum on the subject of planting and sheltering oaks," — " an abstract
of the practice adopted by the government officers in
the national forests " of England, prepared by Alex-
ander Milne.

At first some oaks had been planted by themselves,
and others mixed with Scotch pines; " but in all
cases," says Mr. Milne, " where oaks were planted
actually among the pines, and surrounded by them,
[though the soil might be inferior,] the oaks were
found to be much the best." " For several years past,
the plan pursued has been to plant the inclosures with
Scotch pines only, [a tree very similar to our pitch-
pine,] and when the pines have got to the height of
five or six feet, then to put in good strong oak plants
of about four or five years' growth among the pines,
— not cutting away any pines at first, unless they
happen to be so strong and thick as to overshadow
the oaks. In about two years, it becomes necessary to
shred the branches of the pines, to give light and air
to the oaks, and in about two or three more years to
begin gradually to remove the pines altogether, taking
out a certain number each year, so that, at the end of
twenty or twenty-five years, not a single Scotch pine
shall be left; although, for the first ten or twelve
years, the plantation may have appeared to contain
nothing else but pine. The advantage of this mode
of planting has been found to be that the pines dry
and ameliorate the soil, destroying the coarse grass

and brambles which frequently choke and injure oaks; and that no mending over is necessary, as scarcely an oak so planted is found to fail."

Thus much the English planters have discovered by patient experiment, and, for aught I know, they have taken out a patent for it; but they appear not to have discovered that it was discovered before, and that they are merely adopting the method of Nature, which she long ago made patent to all. She is all the while planting the oaks amid the pines without our knowledge, and at last, instead of government officers, we send a party of wood-choppers to cut down the pines, and so rescue an oak forest, at which we wonder as if it had dropped from the skies.

As I walk amid hickories, even in August, I hear the sound of green pig-nuts falling from time to time, cut off by the chickaree over my head. In the fall, I notice on the ground, either within or in the neighborhood of oak woods, on all sides of the town, stout oak twigs three or four inches long, bearing half-a-dozen empty acorn-cups, which twigs have been gnawed off by squirrels, on both sides of the nuts, in order to make them more portable. The jays scream and the red squirrels scold while you are clubbing and shaking the chestnut-trees, for they are there on the same errand, and two of a trade never agree. I frequently see a red or gray squirrel cast down a green chestnut bur, as I am going through the woods, and I used to think, sometimes, that they were cast at me. In fact, they are so busy about it, in the midst of the chestnut season, that you cannot stand long in the woods without hearing one fall. A sportsman told me that he had, the day before, — that was in the middle of October, — seen a green chestnut bur dropt on our great river meadow, fifty rods from the nearest wood, and much farther from the nearest chestnut-tree, and he could not tell how it came there. Occasionally, when chestnutting in midwinter, I find thirty or forty nuts in a pile, left in its gallery, just under the leaves, by the common wood-mouse.

But especially, in the winter, the extent to which this transportation and planting of nuts is carried on is made apparent by the snow. In almost every wood you will see where the red or gray squirrels have pawed down through the snow in a hundred places, sometimes two feet deep, and almost always directly to a nut or a pine-cone, as directly as if they had started from it and bored upward, — which you and I could not have done. It would be difficult for us to find one before the snow falls. Commonly, no doubt, they had deposited them there in the fall. You wonder if they remember the localities, or discover them by the scent. The red squirrel commonly has its winter abode in the earth under a thicket of evergreens, frequently under a small clump of evergreens in the midst of a deciduous wood. If there are any nut-trees which still retain their nuts, standing at a distance without the wood, their paths often lead directly to and from them. We, therefore, need not suppose an oak standing here and there *in* the wood in order to seed it, but if a few stand within twenty or thirty rods of it, it is sufficient.

I think that I may venture to say that every white-pine cone that falls to the earth naturally in this town, before opening and losing its seeds, and almost every pitch-pine that falls at all, is cut off by a squirrel, and they begin to pluck them long before they are ripe, so that when the crop of white-pine cones is a small one, as it commonly is, they cut off thus almost every one of these before it fairly ripens. I think, moreover, that their design, if I may so speak, in cutting them off green, is, partly, to prevent their opening and losing their seeds, for these are the ones for which they dig through the snow, and the only white-pine cones which contain anything then. I have counted in one heap, within a diameter of four feet, the cores of 239 pitch-pine cones which had been cut off and stripped by the red squirrel the previous winter.

The nuts thus left on the surface, or buried just beneath it, are placed in the most favorable circumstances for germinating. I have sometimes wondered how those which merely fell on the surface of the earth got planted; but, by the end of December, I find the chestnut of the same year partially mixed with the mould, as it were, under the decaying and mouldy leaves, where there is all the moisture and manure they want, for the nuts fall first. In a plentiful year, a large proportion of the nuts are thus covered loosely an inch deep, and are, of course, somewhat concealed from squirrels. One winter, when the crop had been abundant, I got, with the aid of a rake, many quarts of these nuts as late as the tenth of January, and though some bought at the store the same day were more than half of them mouldy, I did not find a single mouldy one among these which I picked from under the wet and mouldy leaves, where they had been snowed on once or twice. Nature knows how to pack them best. They were still plump and tender. Apparently, they do not heat there, though wet. In the spring they were all sprouting.

Loudon says that " when the nut [of the common walnut of Europe] is to be preserved through the winter for the purpose of planting in the following spring, it should be laid in a rot-heap, as soon as gathered, with the husk on, and the heap should be turned over frequently in the course of the winter."

Here, again, he is stealing Nature's " thunder." How can a poor mortal do otherwise? for it is she that finds fingers to steal with, and the treasure to be stolen. In the planting of the seeds of most trees, the best gardeners do no more than follow Nature, though they may not know it. Generally, both large and small ones are most sure to germinate, and succeed best, when only beaten into the earth with the back of a spade, and then covered with leaves or straw. These results to which planters have arrived remind us of the experience of Kane and his companions at the North, who, when learning to live in that climate, were surprised to find themselves steadily adopting the customs of the natives, simply becoming Esquimaux. So, when we experiment in planting forests, we find ourselves at last doing as Nature does. Would it not be well to consult with Nature in the outset? for she is the most extensive and experienced planter of us all, not excepting the Dukes of Athol.[1]

In short, they who have not attended particularly to this subject are but little aware to what an extent quadrupeds and birds are employed, especially in the fall, in collecting, and so disseminating and planting the seeds of trees. It is the almost constant employment of the squirrels at that season, and you rarely

[1] The Dukes of Athol, in Scotland, were famous for their plantations of trees.

meet with one that has not a nut in its mouth, or is not just going to get one. One squirrel-hunter of this town told me that he knew of a walnut-tree which bore particularly good nuts, but that on going to gather them one fall, he found that he had been anticipated by a family of a dozen red squirrels. He took out of the tree, which was hollow, one bushel and three pecks by measurement, without the husks, and they supplied him and his family for the winter. It would be easy to multiply instances of this kind. How commonly in the fall you see the cheek-pouches of the striped squirrel distended by a quantity of nuts! This species gets its scientific name *Tamias*, or the steward, from its habit of storing up nuts and other seeds. Look under a nut-tree a month after the nuts have fallen, and see what proportion of sound nuts to the abortive ones and shells you will find ordinarily. They have been already eaten, or dispersed far and wide. The ground looks like the platform before a grocery, where the gossips of the village sit to crack nuts and less savory jokes. You have come, you would say, after the feast was over, and are presented with the shells only.

Occasionally, when threading the woods in the fall, you will hear a sound as if some one had broken a twig, and, looking up, see a jay pecking at an acorn, or you will see a flock of them at once about it, in the top of an oak, and hear them break them off. They then fly to a suitable limb, and placing the acorn under one foot, hammer away at it busily, making a sound like a woodpecker's tapping, looking round from time to time to see if any foe is approaching, and soon reach the meat, and nibble at it, holding up their heads to swallow, while they hold the

remainder very firmly with their claws. Nevertheless, it often drops to the ground before the bird has
done with it. I can confirm what William Bartram
wrote to Wilson, the ornithologist, that " The jay is
one of the most useful agents in the economy of nature, for disseminating forest trees and other nucifer-
ous and hard-seeded vegetables on which they feed.
Their chief employment during the autumnal season
is foraging to supply their winter stores. In perform-
ing this necessary duty they drop abundance of seed
in their flight over fields, hedges, and by fences, where
they alight to deposit them in the post-holes, etc. It
is remarkable what numbers of young trees rise up in
fields and pastures after a wet winter and spring.
These birds alone are capable, in a few years' time,
to replant all the cleared lands."

I have noticed that squirrels also frequently drop
their nuts in the open land, which will still further
account for the oaks and walnuts which spring up in
pastures, for, depend on it, every new tree comes from
a seed. When I examine the little oaks, one or two
years old, in such places, I invariably find the empty
acorn from which they sprung.

So far from the seed having lain dormant in the
soil since oaks grew there before, as many believe, it
is well known that it is difficult to preserve the vitality of acorns long enough to transport them to Europe ; and it is recommended in Loudon's *Arboretum*,
as the safest course, to sprout them in pots on the
voyage. The same authority states that " very few
acorns of any species will germinate after having been
kept a year," that beechmast " only retains its vital
properties one year," and the black-walnut " seldom
more than six months after it has ripened." I have

frequently found that in November, almost every acorn left on the ground had sprouted or decayed. What with frost, drought, moisture, and worms, the greater part are soon destroyed. Yet it is stated by one botanical writer that " acorns that have lain for centuries, on being ploughed up, have soon vegetated."

Mr. George B. Emerson, in his valuable Report on the Trees and Shrubs of this State, says of the pines : " The tenacity of life of the seeds is remarkable. They will remain for many years unchanged in the ground, protected by the coolness and deep shade of the forest above them. But when the forest is removed, and the warmth of the sun admitted, they immediately vegetate." Since he does not tell us on what observation his remark is founded, I must doubt its truth. Besides, the experience of nurserymen makes it the more questionable.

The stories of wheat raised from seed buried with an ancient Egyptian, and of raspberries raised from seed found in the stomach of a man in England, who is supposed to have died sixteen or seventeen hundred years ago, are generally discredited, simply because the evidence is not conclusive.

Several men of science, Dr. Carpenter among them, have used the statement that beach-plums sprang up in sand which was dug up forty miles inland in Maine, to prove that the seed had lain there a very long time, and some have inferred that the coast has receded so far. But it seems to me necessary to their argument to show, first, that beach-plums grow only on a beach. They are not uncommon here, which is about half that distance from the shore; and I remember a dense patch a few miles north of us, twenty-five miles inland, from which the fruit was annually carried to market. How much further inland they grow, I know not. Dr. Charles T. Jackson speaks of finding "beach-plums" (perhaps they were this kind) more than one hundred miles inland in Maine.

It chances that similar objections lie against all the more notorious instances of the kind on record.

Yet I am prepared to believe that some seeds, especially small ones, may retain their vitality for centuries under favorable circumstances. In the spring of 1859, the old Hunt House, so called, in this town, whose chimney bore the date 1703, was taken down. This stood on land which belonged to John Winthrop, the first governor of Massachusetts, and a part of the house was evidently much older than the above date, and belonged to the Winthrop family. For many years I have ransacked this neighborhood for plants, and I consider myself familiar with its productions. Thinking of the seeds which are said to be sometimes dug up at an unusual depth in the earth, and thus to reproduce long extinct plants, it occurred to me last fall that some new or rare plants might have sprung up in the cellar of this house, which had been covered from the light so long. Searching there on the 22d of September, I found, among other rank weeds, a species of nettle (*Urtica urens*), which I had not found before; dill, which I had not seen growing spontaneously; the Jerusalem oak, which I had seen wild in but one place; black nightshade, which is quite rare hereabouts; and common tobacco, which, though it was often cultivated here in the last century, has for fifty years been an unknown plant in this town, and a few months before this not even I had heard that one man in the north part of the town

was cultivating a few plants for his own use. I have
no doubt that some or all of these plants sprang from
seeds which had long been buried under or about that
house, and that that tobacco is an additional evidence
that the plant was formerly cultivated here. The
cellar has been filled up this year, and four of those
plants, including the tobacco, are now again extinct
in that locality.

It is true, I have shown that the animals consume
a great part of the seeds of trees, and so, at least,
effectually prevent their becoming trees; but in all
these cases, as I have said, the consumer is compelled
to be at the same time the disperser and planter, and
this is the tax which he pays to nature. I think it is
Linnæus who says, that while the swine is rooting
for acorns, he is planting acorns.

Though I do not believe that a plant will spring up
where no seed has been, I have great faith in a seed
—a, to me, equally mysterious origin for it. Con-
vince me that you have a seed there, and I am prepared to expect wonders. I shall even believe that
the millennium is at hand, and that the reign of jus-
tice is about to commence, when the Patent Office, or
Government, begins to distribute, and the people to
plant the seeds of these things.

In the spring of 1857 I planted six seeds sent to
me from the Patent Office, and labelled, I think,
" *Poitrine jaune grosse*," [1] large yellow squash. Two
came up, and one bore a squash which weighed 123½
pounds, the other bore four, weighing together 186¼
pounds. Who would have believed that there was
310 pounds of *poitrine jaune grosse* in that corner of
my garden? These seeds were the bait I used to

[1] Pronounced *pwah-treen zhone groce.*

catch it, my ferrets which I sent into its burrow, my
brace of terriers which unearthed it.   A little mysterious hoeing and manuring was all the *abracadabra*[1]
presto-change that I used, and, lo! true to the label,
they found for me 310 pounds of *poitrine jaune
grosse* there, where it never was known to be, nor
was before.   These talismen had perchance sprung
from America at first, and returned to it with una-
bated force.   The big squash took a premium at your
fair that fall, and I understood that the man who
bought it intended to sell the seeds for ten cents a
piece.   (Were they not cheap at that?)   But I have
more hounds of the same breed.   I learn that one
which I dispatched to a distant town, true to its in-
stincts, points to the large yellow squash there, too,
where no hound ever found it before, as its ancestors
did here and in France.

Other seeds I have which will find other things in
that corner of my garden, in like fashion, almost any
fruit you wish, every year for ages, until the crop
more than fills the whole garden.   You have but little more to do than throw up your cap for entertain-
ment these American days.   Perfect alchemists I keep
who can transmute substances without end, and thus
the corner of my garden is an inexhaustible treasure-
chest.   Here you can dig, not gold, but the value
which gold merely represents; and there is no Signor
Blitz[2] about it.   Yet farmers' sons will stare by the
hour to see a juggler draw ribbons from his throat,
though he tells them it is all deception.   Surely, men
love darkness rather than light.

[1] A charm once used by the superstitious.
[2] A Swiss juggler who was a favorite performer in New England between 1850 and 1860.   His trained canaries were one of
the wonders of the day.

WILD APPLES.

THE HISTORY OF THE APPLE-TREE.

IT is remarkable how closely the history of the Apple-tree is connected with that of man. The geologist tells us that the order of the *Rosaceæ*, which includes the Apple, also the true Grasses, and the *Labiatæ*, or Mints, were introduced only a short time previous to the appearance of man on the globe.

It appears that apples made a part of the food of that unknown primitive people whose traces have lately been found at the bottom of the Swiss lakes, supposed to be older than the foundation of Rome, so old that they had no metallic implements. An entire black and shrivelled Crab-Apple has been recovered from their stores.

Tacitus says of the ancient Germans, that they satisfied their hunger with wild apples, among other things.

Niebuhr[1] observes that "the words for a house, a field, a plough, ploughing, wine, oil, milk, sheep, apples, and others relating to agriculture and the gentler ways of life, agree in Latin and Greek, while the Latin words for all objects pertaining to war or the chase are utterly alien from the Greek." Thus

[1] A German historical critic of ancient life.

the apple-tree may be considered a symbol of peace no less than the olive.

The apple was early so important, and so generally distributed, that its name traced to its root in many languages signifies fruit in general. Μῆλον [Mēlon], in Greek, means an apple, also the fruit of other trees, also a sheep and any cattle, and finally riches in general.

The apple-tree has been celebrated by the Hebrews, Greeks, Romans, and Scandinavians. Some have thought that the first human pair were tempted by its fruit. Goddesses are fabled to have contended for it, dragons were set to watch it, and heroes were employed to pluck it.[1]

The tree is mentioned in at least three places in the Old Testament, and its fruit in two or three more. Solomon sings, " As the apple-tree among the trees of the wood, so is my beloved among the sons." And again, " Stay me with flagons, comfort me with apples." The noblest part of man's noblest feature is named from this fruit, " the apple of the eye."

The apple-tree is also mentioned by Homer and Herodotus. Ulysses saw in the glorious garden of Alcinoüs "pears and pomegranates and apple-trees bearing beautiful fruit." And according to Homer, apples were among the fruits which Tantalus could not pluck, the wind ever blowing their boughs away from him. Theophrastus knew and described the apple-tree as a botanist.

According to the Prose Edda,[2] " Iduna keeps in a box the apples which the gods, when they feel old

---

[1] The Greek myths especially referred to are The Choice of Paris and The Apples of the Hesperides.

[2] The stories of the early Scandinavians.

age approaching, have only to taste of to become young again. It is in this manner that they will be kept in renovated youth until Ragnarök" (or the destruction of the gods).

I learn from Loudon [1] that "the ancient Welsh bards were rewarded for excelling in song by the token of the apple-spray;" and "in the Highlands of Scotland the apple-tree is the badge of the clan Lamont."

The apple-tree belongs chiefly to the northern temperate zone. Loudon says, that "it grows spontaneously in every part of Europe except the frigid zone, and throughout Western Asia, China, and Japan." We have also two or three varieties of the apple indigenous in North America. The cultivated apple-tree was first introduced into this country by the earliest settlers, and is thought to do as well or better here than anywhere else. Probably some of the varieties which are now cultivated were first introduced into Britain by the Romans.

Pliny, adopting the distinction of Theophrastus, says, "Of trees there are some which are altogether wild, some more civilized." Theophrastus includes the apple among the last; and, indeed, it is in this sense the most civilized of all trees. It is as harmless as a dove, as beautiful as a rose, and as valuable as flocks and herds. It has been longer cultivated than any other, and so is more humanized; and who knows but, like the dog, it will at length be no longer traceable to its wild original? It migrates with man, like the dog and horse and cow: first, perchance, from Greece to Italy, thence to England,

[1] An English authority on the culture of orchards and gardens.

thence to America; and our Western emigrant is
still marching steadily toward the setting sun with
the seeds of the apple in his pocket, or perhaps a few
young trees strapped to his load. At least a million
apple-trees are thus set farther westward this year
than any cultivated ones grew last year. Consider
how the Blossom-Week, like the Sabbath, is thus
annually spreading over the prairies; for when man
migrates he carries with him not only his birds,
quadrupeds, insects, vegetables, and his very sward,
but his orchard also.

The leaves and tender twigs are an agreeable food
to many domestic animals, as the cow, horse, sheep,
and goat; and the fruit is sought after by the first,
as well as by the hog. Thus there appears to have
existed a natural alliance between these animals and
this tree from the first. "The fruit of the Crab in
the forests of France" is said to be "a great resource
for the wild-boar."

Not only the Indian, but many indigenous insects,
birds, and quadrupeds, welcomed the apple-tree to
these shores. The tent-caterpillar saddled her eggs
on the very first twig that was formed, and it has
since shared her affections with the wild cherry; and
the canker-worm also in a measure abandoned the
elm to feed on it. As it grew apace, the bluebird,
robin, cherry-bird, king-bird, and many more, came
with haste and built their nests and warbled in its
boughs, and so became orchard-birds, and multiplied
more than ever. It was an era in the history of their
race. The downy woodpecker found such a savory
morsel under its bark, that he perforated it in a ring
quite round the tree before he left it, — a thing
which he had never done before, to my knowledge.

It did not take the partridge long to find out how
sweet its buds were, and every winter eve she flew, and
still flies, from the wood, to pluck them, much to the
farmer's sorrow. The rabbit, too, was not slow to
learn the taste of its twigs and bark; and when the
fruit was ripe, the squirrel half-rolled, half-carried it
to his hole; and even the musquash crept up the
bank from the brook at evening, and greedily de-
voured it, until he had worn a path in the grass
there; and when it was frozen and thawed, the crow
and the jay were glad to taste it occasionally. The
owl crept into the first apple-tree that became hollow,
and fairly hooted with delight, finding it just the
place for him; so, settling down into it, he has re-
mained there ever since.

My theme being the Wild Apple, I will merely
glance at some of the seasons in the annual growth
of the cultivated apple, and pass on to my special
province.

The flowers of the apple are perhaps the most beautiful of any tree, so copious and so delicious to both
sight and scent. The walker is frequently tempted to
turn and linger near some more than usually handsome one, whose blossoms are two thirds expanded.
How superior it is in these respects to the pear, whose
blossoms are neither colored nor fragrant!

By the middle of July, green apples are so large as
to remind us of coddling, and of the autumn. The
sward is commonly strewed with little ones which fall
still-born, as it were, — Nature thus thinning them for
us. The Roman writer Palladius said: "If apples
are inclined to fall before their time, a stone placed in
a split root will retain them." Some such notion, still
surviving, may account for some of the stones which

we see placed to be overgrown in the forks of trees.
They have a saying in Suffolk, England, —

> " At Michaelmas time, or a little before,
> Half an apple goes to the core."

Early apples begin to be ripe about the first of
August; but I think that none of them are so good
to eat as some to smell. One is worth more to scent
your handkerchief with than any perfume which they
sell in the shops. The fragrance of some fruits is not
to be forgotten, along with that of flowers. Some
gnarly apple which I pick up in the road reminds me
by its fragrance of all the wealth of Pomona,[1] — carrying me forward to those days when they will be
collected in golden and ruddy heaps in the orchards
and about the cider-mills.

A week or two later, as you are going by orchards
or gardens, especially in the evenings, you pass through
a little region possessed by the fragrance of ripe apples, and thus enjoy them without price, and without
robbing anybody.

There is thus about all natural products a certain
volatile and ethereal quality which represents their
highest value, and which cannot be vulgarized, or
bought and sold. No mortal has ever enjoyed the
perfect flavor of any fruit, and only the godlike among
men begin to taste its ambrosial qualities. For nectar
and ambrosia are only those fine flavors of every
earthly fruit which our coarse palates fail to perceive,
— just as we occupy the heaven of the gods without
knowing it. When I see a particularly mean man carrying a load of fair and fragrant early apples to market,
I seem to see a contest going on between him and his
horse, on the one side, and the apples on the other,

---

[1] The Roman goddess of fruit and fruit-trees.

and, to my mind, the apples always gain it. Pliny
says that apples are the heaviest of all things, and
that the oxen begin to sweat at the mere sight of a
load of them. Our driver begins to lose his load the
moment he tries to transport them to where they do
not belong, that is, to any but the most beautiful.
Though he gets out from time to time, and feels of
them, and thinks they are all there, I see the stream
of their evanescent and celestial qualities going to
heaven from his cart, while the pulp and skin and
core only are going to market. They are not apples,
but pomace. Are not these still Iduna's apples, the
taste of which keeps the gods forever young? and
think you that they will let Loki or Thjassi carry
them off to Jötunheim,[1] while they grow wrinkled and
gray? No, for Ragnarök, or the destruction of the
gods, is not yet.

There is another thinning of the fruit, commonly
near the end of August or in September, when the
ground is strewn with windfalls; and this happens
especially when high winds occur after rain. In some
orchards you may see fully three quarters of the whole
crop on the ground, lying in a circular form beneath
the trees, yet hard and green, — or, if it is a hillside,
rolled far down the hill. However, it is an ill wind
that blows nobody any good. All the country over,
people are busy picking up the windfalls, and this
will make them cheap for early apple-pies.

In October, the leaves falling, the apples are more
distinct on the trees. I saw one year in a neighboring
town some trees fuller of fruit than I remember to

_____

[1] Jötunheim (*Ye(r)t'-un-hime*) in Scandinavian mythology was
the home of the Jötun or Giants. Loki was a descendant of the
gods, and a companion of the Giants. Thjassi (*Tee-assy*) was a
giant.

have ever seen before, small yellow apples hanging
over the road.   The branches were gracefully droop-
ing with their weight, like a barberry-bush, so that
the whole tree acquired a new character.   Even the
topmost branches, instead of standing erect, spread
and drooped in all directions; and there were so many
poles supporting the lower ones, that they looked like
pictures of banian-trees.   As an old English manuscript says. "The mo appelen the tree bereth the more
sche boweth to the folk."

Surely the apple is the noblest of fruits.   Let the
most beautiful or the swiftest have it.   That should
be the " going " price of apples.

Between the fifth and twentieth of October I see
the barrels lie under the trees.   And perhaps I talk
with one who is selecting some choice barrels to fulfil
an order.   He turns a specked one over many times
before he leaves it out.   If I were to tell what is
passing in my mind, I should say that every one was
specked which he had handled; for he rubs off all
the bloom, and those fugacious ethereal qualities leave
it.   Cool evenings prompt the farmers to make haste,
and at length I see only the ladders here and there
left leaning against the trees.

It would be well if we accepted these gifts with
more joy and gratitude, and did not think it enough
simply to put a fresh load of compost about the tree.
Some old English customs are suggestive at least.   I
find them described chiefly in Brand's " Popular An-
tiquities."   It appears that " on Christmas eve the
farmers and their men in Devonshire take a large
bowl of cider, with a toast in it, and carrying it in
state to the orchard, they salute the apple-trees with
much ceremony, in order to make them bear well the

next season." This salutation consists in " throwing some of the cider about the roots of the tree, placing bits of the toast on the branches," and then, " encircling one of the best bearing trees in the orchard, they drink the following toast three several times : —

> 'Here's to thee, old apple-tree,
> Whence thou mayst bud, and whence thou mayst blow,
> And whence thou mayst bear apples enow !
> Hats-full ! caps-full !
> Bushel, bushel, sacks-full !
> And my pockets full, too ! Hurra !' "

Also what was called " apple-howling " used to be practised in various counties of England on New-Year's eve. A troop of boys visited the different orchards, and, encircling the apple-trees, repeated the following words : —

> " Stand fast, root ! bear well, top !
> Pray God send us a good howling **crop** :
> Every twig, apples big ;
> Every bow, apples enow ! "

" They then shout in chorus, one of the boys **accompanying** them on a cow's horn. During this ceremony they rap the trees with their sticks." This is called " wassailing " the trees, and is thought by some to be " a relic of the heathen sacrifice to Pomona."

Herrick sings, —

> " Wassaile the trees that they may beare
> You many a plum and many a peare ;
> For more or less fruits they will bring
> As you so give them wassailing."

Our poets have as yet a better right to sing of cider than of wine ; but it behooves them to sing better **than** English Phillips did, else they will do no credit to their Muse.

THE WILD APPLE.

So much for the more civilized apple-trees (*urba-niores*, as Pliny calls them). I love better to go through the old orchards of ungrafted apple-trees, at whatever season of the year, — so irregularly planted: sometimes two trees standing close together; and the rows so devious that you would think that they not only had grown while the owner was sleeping, but had been set out by him in a somnambulic state. The rows of grafted fruit will never tempt me to wander amid them like these. But I now, alas, speak rather from memory than from any recent experience, such ravages have been made!

Some soils, like a rocky tract called the Easter-brooks Country in my neighborhood, are so suited to the apple, that it will grow faster in them without any care, or if only the ground is broken up once a year, than it will in many places with any amount of care. The owners of this tract allow that the soil is excellent for fruit, but they say that it is so rocky that they have not patience to plough it, and that, together with the distance, is the reason why it is not cultivated. There are, or were recently, extensive orchards there standing without order. Nay, they spring up wild and bear well there in the midst of pines, birches, maples, and oaks. I am often surprised to see rising amid these trees the rounded tops of apple-trees glowing with red or yellow fruit, in harmony with the autumnal tints of the forest.

Going up the side of a cliff about the first of November. I saw a vigorous young apple-tree, which, planted by birds or cows, had shot up amid the rocks and open woods there, and had now much fruit on it,

uninjured by the frosts, when all cultivated apples were
gathered. It was a rank wild growth, with many green
leaves on it still, and made an impression of thorniness. The fruit was hard and green, but looked as if
it would be palatable in the winter. Some was dangling on the twigs, but more half-buried in the wet
leaves under the tree, or rolled far down the hill amid
the rocks. The owner knows nothing of it. The
day was not observed when it first blossomed, nor
when it first bore fruit, unless by the chickadee.
There was no dancing on the green beneath it in its
honor, and now there is no hand to pluck its fruit, —
which is only gnawed by squirrels, as I perceive. It
has done double duty, — not only borne this crop, but
each twig has grown a foot into the air. And this is
such fruit! bigger than many berries, we must admit,
and carried home will be sound and palatable next
spring. What care I for Iduna's apples so long as I
can get these?

When I go by this shrub thus late and hardy, and
see its dangling fruit, I respect the tree, and I am
grateful for Nature's bounty, even though I cannot
eat it. Here on this rugged and woody hillside has
grown an apple-tree, not planted by man, no relic of
a former orchard, but a natural growth, like the pines
and oaks. Most fruits which we prize and use depend entirely on our care. Corn and grain, potatoes,
peaches, melons, etc., depend altogether on our planting; but the apple emulates man's independence and
enterprise. It is not simply carried, as I have said,
but, like him, to some extent, it has migrated to this
New World, and is even, here and there, making its
way amid the aboriginal trees; just as the ox and
dog and horse sometimes run wild and maintain themselves.

Even the sourest and crabbedest apple, growing in the most unfavorable position, suggests such thoughts as these, it is so noble a fruit.

THE CRAB.

. Nevertheless, *our* wild apple is wild only like myself, perchance, who belong not to the aboriginal race here, but have strayed into the woods from the cultivated stock. Wilder still, as I have said, there grows elsewhere in this country a native and aboriginal Crab-Apple, " whose nature has not yet been modified by cultivation." It is found from Western New York to Minnesota and southward. Michaux [1] says that its ordinary height " is fifteen or eighteen feet, but it is sometimes found twenty-five or thirty feet high," and that the large ones " exactly resemble the common apple-tree." " The flowers are white mingled with rose-color, and are collected in corymbs." They are remarkable for their delicious odor. The fruit, according to him, is about an inch and a half in diameter, and is intensely acid. Yet they make fine sweet-meats, and also cider of them. He concludes, that " if, on being cultivated, it does not yield new and palatable varieties, it will at least be celebrated for the beauty of its flowers, and for the sweetness of its perfume."

I never saw the Crab-Apple till May, 1861. I had heard of it through Michaux, but more modern botanists, so far as I know, have not treated it as of any peculiar importance. Thus it was a half-fabulous tree to me. I contemplated a pilgrimage to the " Glades," a portion of Pennsylvania, where it was said to grow to perfection. I thought of sending to

[1] Pronounced *mee-shō'*, a French botanist and traveller.

a nursery for it, but doubted if they had it, or would
distinguish it from European varieties. At last I had
occasion to go to Minnesota, and on entering Michi-
gan I began to notice from the cars a tree with handsome rose-colored flowers. At first I thought it some
variety of thorn ; but it was not long before the truth
flashed on me, that this was my long-sought Crab-
Apple. It was the prevailing flowering shrub or tree
to be seen from the cars at that season of the year, —
about the middle of May. But the cars never stopped
before one, and so I was launched on the bosom of
the Mississippi without having touched one, experienc-
ing the fate of Tantalus. On arriving at St. An-
thony's Falls, I was sorry to be told that I was too
far north for the Crab-Apple. Nevertheless I succeeded in finding it about eight miles west of the
Falls ; touched it and smelled it, and secured a linger-
ing corymb of flowers for my herbarium. This must
have been near its northern limit.

HOW THE WILD APPLE GROWS.

But though these are indigenous, like the Indians,
I doubt whether they are any hardier than those back-
woodsmen among the apple-trees, which, though de-
scended from cultivated stocks, plant themselves in
distant fields and forests, where the soil is favorable
to them. I know of no trees which have more difficulties to contend with, and which more sturdily
resist their foes. These are the ones whose story we
have to tell. It oftentimes reads thus : —

Near the beginning of May, we notice little thickets
of apple-trees just springing up in the pastures where
cattle have been, — as the rocky ones of our Easter-
brooks Country, or the top of Nobscot Hill in Sud-

bury.   One or two of these perhaps survive the
drought and other accidents, — their very birthplace
defending them against the encroaching grass and
some other dangers, at first.

> In two years' time 't had thus
>   Reached the level of the rocks,
> Admired the stretching world,
>   Nor feared the wandering flocks.
>
> But at this tender age
>   Its sufferings began :
> There came a browsing ox
>   And cut it down a span.

This time, perhaps, the ox does not notice it amid the
grass ; but the next year, when it has grown more
stout, he recognizes it for a fellow-emigrant from the
old country, the flavor of whose leaves and twigs he
well knows ; and though at first he pauses to welcome
it, and express his surprise, and gets for answer, " The
same cause that brought you here brought me," he
nevertheless browses it again, reflecting, it may be,
that he has some title to it.

Thus cut down annually, it does not despair ; but,
putting forth two short twigs for every one cut off, it
spreads out low along the ground in the hollows or
between the rocks, growing more stout and scrubby,
until it forms, not a tree as yet, but a little pyramidal,
stiff, twiggy mass, almost as solid and impenetrable
as a rock.   Some of the densest and most impenetrable clumps of bushes that I have ever seen, as well
on account of the closeness and stubbornness of their
branches as of their thorns, have been these wild-apple
scrubs.   They are more like the scrubby fir and black
spruce on which you stand, and sometimes walk, on
the tops of mountains, where cold is the demon they

contend with, than anything else. No wonder they
are prompted to grow thorns at last, to defend themselves against such foes. In their thorniness, however, there is no malice, only some malic acid.

The rocky pastures of the tract I have referred to
— for they maintain their ground best in a rocky
field — are thickly sprinkled with these little tufts,
reminding you often of some rigid gray mosses or
lichens, and you see thousands of little trees just
springing up between them, with the seed still at-
tached to them.

Being regularly clipped all around each year by the
cows, as a hedge with shears, they are often of a perfect conical or pyramidal form, from one to four feet
high, and more or less sharp, as if trimmed by the
gardener's art. In the pastures on Nobscot Hill and
its spurs they make fine dark shadows when the sun is
low. They are also an excellent covert from hawks
for many small birds that roost and build in them.
Whole flocks perch in them at night, and I have seen
three robins' nests in one which was six feet in diameter.

No doubt many of these are already old trees, if
you reckon from the day they were planted, but in-
fants still when you consider their development and
the long life before them. I counted the annual rings
of some which were just one foot high, and as wide as
high, and found that they were about twelve years
old, but quite sound and thrifty! They were so low
that they were unnoticed by the walker, while many
of their contemporaries from the nurseries were already bearing considerable crops. But what you gain
in time is perhaps in this case, too, lost in power, —
that is, in the vigor of the tree. This is their pyramidal state.

The cows continue to browse them thus for twenty years or more, keeping them down and compelling them to spread, until at last they are so broad that they become their own fence, when some interior shoot, which their foes cannot reach, darts upward with joy: for it has not forgotten its high calling, and bears its own peculiar fruit in triumph.

Such are the tactics by which it finally defeats its bovine foes. Now, if you have watched the progress of a particular shrub, you will see that it is no longer a simple pyramid or cone, but out of its apex there rises a sprig or two, growing more lustily perchance than an orchard-tree, since the plant now devotes the whole of its repressed energy to these upright parts. In a short time these become a small tree, an inverted pyramid resting on the apex of the other, so that the whole has now the form of a vast hour-glass. The spreading bottom, having served its purpose, finally disappears, and the generous tree permits the now harmless cows to come in and stand in its shade, and rub against and redden its trunk, which has grown in spite of them, and even to taste a part of its fruit, and so disperse the seed.

Thus the cows create their own shade and food; and the tree, its hour-glass being inverted, lives a second life, as it were.

It is an important question with some nowadays, whether you should trim young apple-trees as high as your nose or as high as your eyes. The ox trims them up as high as he can reach, and that is about the right height, I think.

In spite of wandering kine and other adverse cir-cumstances, that despised shrub, valued only by small birds as a covert and shelter from hawks, has its blossom-week at last, and in course of time its harvest, sincere, though small.

By the end of some October, when its leaves have fallen, I frequently see such a central sprig, whose progress I have watched, when I thought it had forgotten its destiny, as I had, bearing its first crop of small green or yellow or rosy fruit, which the cows cannot get at over the bushy and thorny hedge which surrounds it, and I make haste to taste the new and undescribed variety. We have all heard of the numerous varieties of fruit invented by Van Mons [1] and Knight.[2] This is the system of Van Cow, and she has invented far more and more memorable varieties than both of them.

Through what hardships it may attain to bear a sweet fruit! Though somewhat small, it may prove equal, if not superior, in flavor to that which has grown in a garden, — will perchance be all the sweeter and more palatable for the very difficulties it has had to contend with. Who knows but this chance wild fruit, planted by a cow or a bird on some remote and rocky hillside, where it is as yet unobserved by man, may be the choicest of all its kind, and foreign potentates shall hear of it, and royal societies seek to propagate it, though the virtues of the perhaps truly crabbed owner of the soil may never be heard of, — at least, beyond the limits of his village? It was thus the Porter and the Baldwin grew.

Every wild-apple shrub excites our expectation thus, somewhat as every wild child. It is, perhaps, a prince in disguise. What a lesson to man! So are human beings, referred to the highest standard, the

[1] A Belgian chemist and horticulturist.
[2] An English vegetable physiologist.

celestial fruit which they suggest and aspire to bear, browsed on by fate; and only the most persistent and strongest genius defends itself and prevails, sends a tender scion upward at last, and drops its perfect fruit on the ungrateful earth. Poets and philosophers and statesmen thus spring up in the country pastures, and outlast the hosts of unoriginal men.

Such is always the pursuit of knowledge. The celestial fruits, the golden apples of the Hesperides, are ever guarded by a hundred-headed dragon which never sleeps, so that it is an herculean labor to pluck them.

This is one and the most remarkable way in which the wild apple is propagated; but commonly it springs up at wide intervals in woods and swamps, and by the sides of roads, as the soil may suit it, and grows with comparative rapidity. Those which grow in dense woods are very tall and slender. I frequently pluck from these trees a perfectly mild and tamed fruit. As Palladius says, " And the ground is strewn with the fruit of an unbidden apple-tree."

It is an old notion, that, if these wild trees do not bear a valuable fruit of their own, they are the best stock by which to transmit to posterity the most highly prized qualities of others. However, I am not in search of stocks, but the wild fruit itself, whose fierce gust has suffered no " inteneration." It is not my

> " highest plot
> To plant the Bergamot."

THE FRUIT, AND ITS FLAVOR.

The time for wild apples is the last of October and the first of November. They then get to be palatable, for they ripen late, and they are still, perhaps, as beautiful as ever. I make a great account of these fruits, which the farmers do not think it worth the while to gather, — wild flavors of the Muse, vivacious and inspiriting. The farmer thinks that he has better in his barrels; but he is mistaken, unless he has a walker's appetite and imagination, neither of which can he have.

Such as grow quite wild, and are left out till the first of November, I presume that the owner does not mean to gather. They belong to children as wild as themselves, — to certain active boys that I know, — to the wild-eyed woman of the fields, to whom nothing comes amiss, who gleans after all the world, — and, moreover, to us walkers. We have met with them, and they are ours. These rights, long enough insisted upon, have come to be an institution in some old countries, where they have learned how to live. I hear that " the custom of grippling, which may be called apple-gleaning, is, or was formerly, practised in Herefordshire. It consists in leaving a few apples, which are called the gripples, on every tree, after the general gathering, for the boys, who go with climbing-poles and bags to collect them."

As for those I speak of, I pluck them as a wild fruit, native to this quarter of the earth, — fruit of old trees that have been dying ever since I was a boy and are not yet dead, frequented only by the wood-pecker and the squirrel, deserted now by the owner, who has not faith enough to look under their boughs. From the appearance of the tree-top, at a little distance, you would expect nothing but lichens to drop from it, but your faith is rewarded by finding the ground strewn with spirited fruit, — some of it, perhaps, collected at squirrel-holes, with the marks of

their teeth by which they carried them, — some containing a cricket or two silently feeding within, and
some, especially in damp days, a shell-less snail. The
very sticks and stones lodged in the tree-top might
have convinced you of the savoriness of the fruit
which has been so eagerly sought after in past years.

I have seen no account of these among the " Fruits
and Fruit-Trees of America," though they are more
memorable to my taste than the grafted kinds; more
racy and wild American flavors do they possess, when
October and November, when December and January,
and perhaps February and March even, have assuaged
them somewhat. An old farmer in my neighborhood,
who always selects the right word, says that "they
have a kind of bow-arrow tang."

Apples for grafting appear to have been selected
commonly, not so much for their spirited flavor, as
for their mildness, their size, and bearing qualities, —
not so much for their beauty, as for their fairness and
soundness. Indeed, I have no faith in the selected
lists of pomological gentlemen. Their " Favorites "
and " Non-suches " and " Seek-no-farthers," when I
have fruited them, commonly turn out very tame and
forgetable. They are eaten with comparatively little
zest, and have no real *tang* nor *smack* to them.

What if some of these wildings are acrid and puck-
ery, genuine *verjuice*, do they not still belong to the
Pomaceæ, which are uniformly innocent and kind to
our race? I still begrudge them to the cider-mill.
Perhaps they are not fairly ripe yet.

No wonder that these small and high-colored apples
are thought to make the best cider. Loudon quotes
from the " Herefordshire Report," that " apples of a
small size are always, if equal in quality, to be pre-

ferred to those of a larger size, in order that the rind
and kernel may bear the greatest proportion to the
pulp, which affords the weakest and most watery
juice." And he says, that, "to prove this, Dr. Sy-
monds, of Hereford, about the year 1800, made one
hogshead of cider entirely from the rinds and cores
of apples, and another from the pulp only, when the
first was found of extraordinary strength and flavor
while the latter was sweet and insipid."

Evelyn [1] says that the "Red-strake" was the favorite cider-apple in his day; and he quotes one Dr.
Newburg as saying, "In Jersey 't is a general observation, as I hear, that the more of red any apple has
in its rind, the more proper it is for this use. Pale-
faced apples they exclude as much as may be from
their cider-vat." This opinion still prevails.

All apples are good in November. Those which
the farmer leaves out as unsalable, and unpalatable
to those who frequent the markets, are choicest fruit
to the walker. But it is remarkable that the wild
apple, which I praise as so spirited and racy when
eaten in the fields or woods, being brought into the
house, has frequently a harsh and crabbed taste. The
Saunterer's Apple not even the saunterer can eat in
the house. The palate rejects it there, as it does haws
and acorns, and demands a tamed one; for there you
miss the November air, which is the sauce it is to be
eaten with. Accordingly, when Tityrus, seeing the
lengthening shadows, invites Meliboeus to go home
and pass the night with him, he promises him *mild*
apples and soft chestnuts. I frequently pluck wild
apples of so rich and spicy a flavor that I wonder all
orchardists do not get a scion from that tree, and I

---

[1] An English writer of the seventeenth century.

fail not to bring home my pockets full.   But perchance, when I take one out of my desk and taste it
in my chamber I find it unexpectedly crude, — sour
enough to set a squirrel's teeth on edge and make a
jay scream.

These apples have hung in the wind and frost and
rain till they have absorbed the qualities of the weather
or season, and thus are highly *seasoned*, and they
pierce and *sting* and *permeate* us with their spirit.
They must be eaten in *season*, accordingly, — that is,
out-of-doors.

To appreciate the wild and sharp flavors of these
October fruits, it is necessary that you be breathing
the sharp October or November air.   The out-door
air and exercise which the walker gets give a different tone to his palate, and he craves a fruit which the
sedentary would call harsh and crabbed.   They must
be eaten in the fields, when your system is all aglow
with exercise, when the frosty weather nips your fingers, the wind rattles the bare boughs or rustles the
few remaining leaves, and the jay is heard screaming
around.   What is sour in the house a bracing walk
makes sweet.   Some of these apples might be labelled,
" To be eaten in the wind."

Of course no flavors are thrown away; they are intended for the taste that is up to them.   Some apples
have two distinct flavors, and perhaps one-half of
them must be eaten in the house, the other out-
doors.   One Peter Whitney wrote from Northborough
in 1782, for the Proceedings of the Boston Academy, describing an apple-tree in that town " produc-
ing fruit of opposite qualities, part of the same apple
being frequently sour and the other sweet ; " also some
all sour, and others all sweet, and this diversity on all
parts of the tree.

There is a wild apple on Nawshawtuck Hill in my town which has to me a peculiarly pleasant bitter tang, not perceived till it is three-quarters tasted. It remains on the tongue. As you eat it, it smells exactly like a squash-bug. It is a sort of triumph to eat and relish it.

I hear that the fruit of a kind of plum-tree in Provence is "called *Prunes sibarelles*, because it is impossible to whistle after having eaten them, from their sourness." But perhaps they were only eaten in the house and in summer, and if tried out-of-doors in a stinging atmosphere, who knows but you could whistle an octave higher and clearer?

In the fields only are the sours and bitters of Nature appreciated; just as the wood-chopper eats his meal in a sunny glade, in the middle of a winter day, with content, basks in a sunny ray there, and dreams of summer in a degree of cold which, experienced in a chamber, would make a student miserable. They who are at work abroad are not cold, but rather it is they who sit shivering in houses. As with temperatures, so with flavors; as with cold and heat, so with sour and sweet. This natural raciness, the sours and bitters which the diseased palate refuses, are the true condiments.

Let your condiments be in the condition of your senses. To appreciate the flavor of these wild apples requires vigorous and healthy senses, *papillæ*[1] firm and erect on the tongue and palate, not easily flattened and tamed.

From my experience with wild apples, I can understand that there may be reason for a savage's prefer-

[1] A Latin word, accent on the second syllable, meaning here the rough surface of the tongue and palate.

ring many kinds of food which the civilized man rejects. The former has the palate of an out-door man. It takes a savage or wild taste to appreciate a wild fruit.

What a healthy out-of-door appetite it takes to relish the apple of life, the apple of the world, then!

> "Nor is it every apple I desire,
>   Nor that which pleases every palate best ;
> 'T is not the lasting Deuxan I require,
>   Nor yet the red-cheeked Greening I request,
> Nor that which first beshrewed the name of wife,
> Nor that whose beauty caused the golden strife :
> No, no ! bring me an apple from the tree of life."

So there is one *thought* for the field, another for the house. I would have my thoughts, like wild apples, to be food for walkers, and will not warrant them to be palatable, if tasted in the house.

THEIR BEAUTY.

Almost all wild apples are handsome. They cannot be too gnarly and crabbed and rusty to look at. The gnarliest will have some redeeming traits even to the eye. You will discover some evening redness dashed or sprinkled on some protuberance or in some cavity. It is rare that the summer lets an apple go without streaking or spotting it on some part of its sphere. It will have some red stains, commemorating the mornings and evenings it has witnessed; some dark and rusty blotches, in memory of the clouds and foggy, mildewy days that have passed over it; and a spacious field of green reflecting the general face of Nature, — green even as the fields; or a yellow ground, which implies a milder flavor, — yellow as the harvest, or russet as the hills.

Apples, these I mean, unspeakably fair, — apples not of Discord, but of Concord! Yet not so rare but that the homeliest may have a share. Painted by the frosts, some a uniform clear bright yellow, or red, or crimson, as if their spheres had regularly revolved, and enjoyed the influence of the sun on all sides alike, — some with the faintest pink blush imaginable, — some brindled with deep red streaks like a cow, or with hundreds of fine blood-red rays running regularly from the stem-dimple to the blossom-end, like meridional lines, on a straw-colored ground, — some touched with a greenish rust, like a fine lichen, here and there, with crimson blotches or eyes more or less confluent and fiery when wet, — and others gnarly, and freckled or peppered all over on the stem side with fine crimson spots on a white ground, as if accidentally sprinkled from the brush of Him who paints the autumn leaves. Others, again, are sometimes red inside, perfused with a beautiful blush, fairy food, too beautiful to eat, — apple of the Hesperides, apple of the evening sky! But like shells and pebbles on the sea-shore, they must be seen as they sparkle amid the withering leaves in some dell in the woods, in the autumnal air, or as they lie in the wet grass, and not when they have wilted and faded in the house.

THE NAMING OF THEM.

It would be a pleasant pastime to find suitable names for the hundred varieties which go to a single heap at the cider-mill. Would it not tax a man's invention, — no one to be named after a man, and all in the *lingua vernacula?*[1] Who shall stand godfather

---

[1] *Lingua verna'cula*, common speech.

at the christening of the wild apples? It would exhaust the Latin and Greek languages, if they were used, and make the *lingua vernacula* flag. We should have to call in the sunrise and the sunset, the rainbow and the autumn woods and the wild flowers, and the woodpecker and the purple finch, and the squirrel and the jay and the butterfly, the November traveller and the truant boy, to our aid.

In 1836 there were in the garden of the London Horticultural Society more than fourteen hundred distinct sorts. But here are species which they have not in their catalogue, not to mention the varieties which our Crab might yield to cultivation.

Let us enumerate a few of these. I find myself compelled, after all, to give the Latin names of some for the benefit of those who live where English is not spoken, — for they are likely to have a world-wide reputation.

There is, first of all, the Wood-Apple (*Malus sylvatica*); the Blue-Jay Apple; the Apple which grows in Dells in the Woods (*sylvestrivallis*), also in Hollows in Pastures (*campestrivallis*); the Apple that grows in an old Cellar-Hole (*Malus cellaris*); the Meadow-Apple; the Partridge-Apple; the Truant's Apple (*Cessatoris*), which no boy will ever go by without knocking off some, however *late* it may be; the Saunterer's Apple, — you must lose yourself before you can find the way to that; the Beauty of the Air (*Decus Aëris*); December-Eating; the Frozen-Thawed (*gelato-soluta*), good only in that state; the Concord Apple, possibly the same with the *Musketa-quidensis;* the Assabet Apple; the Brindled Apple; Wine of New England; the Chickaree Apple; the Green Apple (*Malus viridis*); — this has many synonyms; in an imperfect state, it is the *Cholera morbifera aut dysenterifera, puerulis dilectissima ;* [1] — the Apple which Atalanta stopped to pick up; the Hedge-Apple (*Malus Sepium*); the Slug-Apple (*limacea*) ; the Railroad-Apple, which perhaps came from a core thrown out of the cars; the Apple whose Fruit we tasted in our Youth; our Particular Apple, not to be found in any catalogue, — *Pedestrium Solatium ;* [2] also the Apple where hangs the Forgotten Scythe; Iduna's Apples, and the Apples which Loki found in the Wood ; and a great many more I have on my list, too numerous to mention, — all of them good. As Bodæus exclaims, referring to the cultivated kinds, and adapting Virgil to his case, so I, adapting Bodæus, —

" Not if I had a hundred tongues, a hundred mouths,
  An iron voice, could I describe all the forms
  And reckon up all the names of these *wild apples.*"

THE LAST GLEANING.

By the middle of November the wild apples have lost some of their brilliancy, and have chiefly fallen. A great part are decayed on the ground, and the sound ones are more palatable than before. The note of the chickadee sounds now more distinct, as you wander amid the old trees, and the autumnal dandelion is half-closed and tearful. But still, if you are a skilful gleaner, you may get many a pocket-full even of grafted fruit, long after apples are supposed to be gone out-of-doors. I know a Blue-Pearmain tree, growing within the edge of a swamp, almost as

[1] The apple that brings the disease of cholera and of dysentery, the fruit that small boys like best.
[2] The tramp's comfort.

good as wild. You would not suppose that there was
any fruit left there, on the first survey, but you must
look according to system. Those which lie exposed
are quite brown and rotten now, or perchance a few
still show one blooming cheek here and there amid
the wet leaves. Nevertheless, with experienced eyes,
I explore amid the bare alders and the huckleberry-
bushes and the withered sedge, and in the crevices of
the rocks, which are full of leaves, and pry under the
fallen and decaying ferns, which, with apple and
alder leaves, thickly strew the ground. For I know
that they lie concealed, fallen into hollows long since
and covered up by the leaves of the tree itself, — a
proper kind of packing. From these lurking-places,
anywhere within the circumference of the tree, I
draw forth the fruit, all wet and glossy, maybe nib-
bled by rabbits and hollowed out by crickets and
perhaps with a leaf or two cemented to it (as Curzon [1]
an old manuscript from a monastery's mouldy cellar),
but still with a rich bloom on it, and at least as ripe
and well kept, if not better than those in barrels,
more crisp and lively than they. If these resources
fail to yield anything, I have learned to look between
the bases of the suckers which spring thickly from
some horizontal limb, for now and then one lodges
there, or in the very midst of an alder-clump, where
they are covered by leaves, safe from cows which may
have smelled them out. If I am sharp-set, for I do
not refuse the Blue-Pearmain, I fill my pockets on
each side; and as I retrace my steps in the frosty
eve, being perhaps four or five miles from home, I

[1] Robert Curzon was a traveller who searched for old manuscripts in the monasteries of the Levant. See his book, *Ancient Monasteries of the East.*

eat one first from this side, and then from that, to keep my balance.

I learn from Topsell's Gesner, whose authority appears to be Albertus, that the following is the way in which the hedgehog collects and carries home his apples. He says: "His meat is apples, worms, or grapes: when he findeth apples or grapes on the earth, he rolleth himself upon them, until he have filled all his prickles, and then carrieth them home to his den, never bearing above one in his mouth; and if it fortune that one of them fall off by the way, he likewise shaketh off all the residue, and walloweth upon them afresh, until they be all settled upon his back again. So, forth he goeth, making a noise like a cart-wheel; and if he have any young ones in his nest, they pull off his load wherewithal he is loaded, eating thereof what they please, and laying up the residue for the time to come."

THE "FROZEN-THAWED" APPLE.

Toward the end of November, though some of the sound ones are yet more mellow and perhaps more edible, they have generally, like the leaves, lost their beauty, and are beginning to freeze. It is finger-cold, and prudent farmers get in their barrelled apples, and bring you the apples and cider which they have engaged; for it is time to put them into the cellar. Perhaps a few on the ground show their red cheeks above the early snow, and occasionally some even preserve their color and soundness under the snow throughout the winter. But generally at the beginning of the winter they freeze hard, and soon, though undecayed, acquire the color of a baked apple.

Before the end of December, generally, they ex-

perience their first thawing. Those which a month
ago were sour, crabbed, and quite unpalatable to the
civilized taste, such at least as were frozen while
sound, let a warmer sun come to thaw them, for they
are extremely sensitive to its rays, are found to be
filled with a rich, sweet cider, better than any bottled
cider that I know of, and with which I am better
acquainted than with wine. All apples are good in
this state, and your jaws are the cider-press. Others,
which have more substance, are a sweet and luscious
food, — in my opinion of more worth than the pine-
apples which are imported from the West Indies.
Those which lately even I tasted only to repent of it,
— for I am semi-civilized, — which the farmer willingly left on the tree, I am now glad to find have
the property of hanging on like the leaves of the
young oaks. It is a way to keep cider sweet without
boiling. Let the frost come to freeze them first,
solid as stones, and then the rain or a warm winter
day to thaw them, and they will seem to have borrowed a flavor from heaven through the medium of
the air in which they hang. Or perchance you find,
when you get home, that those which rattled in your
pocket have thawed, and the ice is turned to cider.
But after the third or fourth freezing and thawing
they will not be found so good.

What are the imported half-ripe fruits of the torrid
South to this fruit matured by the cold of the frigid
North? These are those crabbed apples with which
I cheated my companion, and kept a smooth face that
I might tempt him to eat. Now we both greedily
fill our pockets with them, — bending to drink the
cup and save our lappets from the overflowing juice,
— and grow more social with their wine. Was there

one that hung so high and sheltered by the tangled branches that our sticks could not dislodge it?

It is a fruit never carried to market, that I am aware of, — quite distinct from the apple of the markets, as from dried apple and cider, — and it is not every winter that produces it in perfection.

The era of the Wild Apple will soon be past. It is a fruit which will probably become extinct in New England. You may still wander through old orchards of native fruit of great extent, which for the most part went to the cider-mill, now all gone to decay. I have heard of an orchard in a distant town, on the side of a hill, where the apples rolled down and lay four feet deep against a wall on the lower side, and this the owner cut down for fear they should be made into cider. Since the temperance reform and the general introduction of grafted fruit, no native apple-trees, such as I see everywhere in deserted pastures, and where the woods have grown up around them, are set out. I fear that he who walks over these fields a century hence will not know the pleasure of knocking off wild apples. Ah, poor man, there are many pleasures which he will not know! Notwithstanding the prevalence of the Baldwin and the Porter, I doubt if so extensive orchards are set out to-day in my town as there were a century ago, when those vast straggling cider-orchards were planted, when men both ate and drank apples, when the pomace-heap was the only nursery, and trees cost nothing but the trouble of setting them out. Men could afford then to stick a tree by every wall-side and let it take its chance. I see nobody planting trees to-day in such out-of-the-way places, along the lonely roads and lanes, and at the bottom of dells in the wood. Now that they have grafted trees, and pay a price for them, they collect them into a plat by their houses, and fence them in, — and the end of it all will be that we shall be compelled to look for our apples in a barrel.

This is " The word of the Lord that came to Joel the son of Pethuel.

" Hear this, ye old men, and give ear, all ye inhabitants of the land! Hath this been in your days, or even in the days of your fathers ? . . .

" That which the palmer-worm hath left hath the locust eaten ; and that which the locust hath left hath the canker-worm eaten ; and that which the canker-worm hath left hath the caterpillar eaten.

" Awake, ye drunkards, and weep ! and howl, all ye drinkers of wine, because of the new wine ! for it is cut off from your mouth.

" For a nation is come up upon my land, strong, and without number, whose teeth are the teeth of a lion, and he hath the cheek-teeth of a great lion.

" He hath laid my vine waste, and barked my fig-tree ; he hath made it clean bare, and cast it away ; the branches thereof are made white. . . .

" Be ye ashamed, O ye husbandmen ! howl, O ye vine-dressers ! . . .

" The vine is dried up, and the fig-tree languisheth ; the pomegranate-tree, the palm-tree also, and the apple-tree, even all the trees of the field, are withered : because joy is withered away from the sons of men." [1]

[1] JOEL, chapter i., verses 1–12.

Printed in the United States
144055LV00006B/22/A